Foundation Borders

Hall & Haywood

Jane Hall & Dixie Haywood

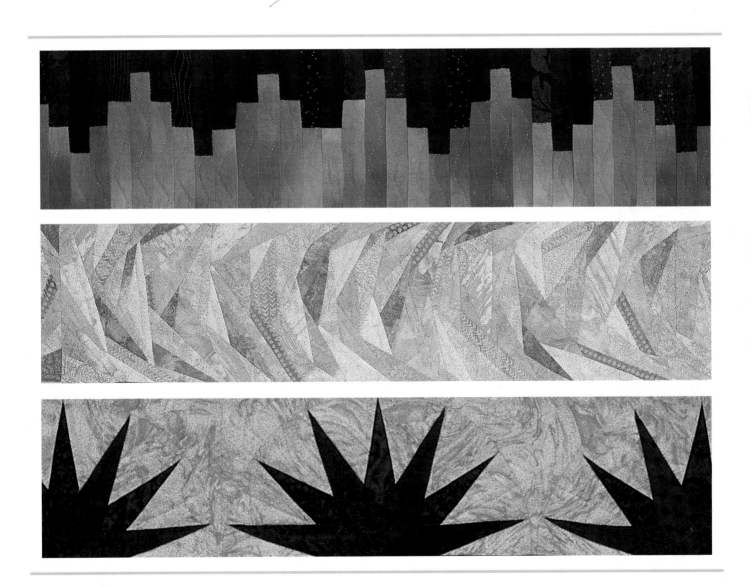

American Quilter's Society
P. O. Box 3290 • Paducah, KY 42002-3290
www.AQSquilt.com

Located in Paducah, Kentucky, the American Quilter's Society (AQS) is dedicated to promoting the accomplishments of today's quilters. Through its publications and events, AQS strives to honor today's quiltmakers and their work and to inspire future creativity and innovation in quiltmaking.

EDITOR: BARBARA SMITH

GRAPHIC DESIGN: ELAINE WILSON

COVER DESIGN: MICHAEL BUCKINGHAM

PHOTOGRAPHY: CHARLES R. LYNCH, UNLESS OTHERWISE STATED

   PHOTOS BY MELLISA KARLIN MAHONEY COURTESY OF QUILTER'S NEWSLETTER MAGAZINE

Library of Congress Cataloging-in-Publication Data

Hall, Jane, 1932–

   Foundation borders: Hall and Haywood / by Jane Hall and Dixie Haywood

      p. cm.

      ISBN 1-57432-801-8

   1. Quilting--Patterns. 2. Patchwork--Patterns. 3. Patchwork quilts.
   4. Borders, Ornamental (Decorative arts)   I. Haywood, Dixie. II.
   American Quilter's Society. III. Title.

   TT835 .H33194 2002
   746.46--dc21

                              2002014340

Additional copies of this book may be ordered from the American Quilter's Society, PO Box 3290, Paducah, KY 42002-3290, or online at www.AQSquilt.com.

Dedication

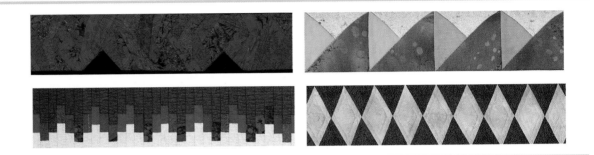

Dixie dedicates this book to the memory of her mother, Rosalie Mae Revie Hamer, whose creativity enriched the lives of friends and family.

Jane dedicates this book to her mother and grandmothers, who gave her the foundations for working with both her hands and her heart in the sewing arts.

Contents

Introduction

It is a rare quilt that doesn't benefit from a well thought-out border. The frame a border provides can put "finis" on the quilt. It completes the overall design, emphasizing colors and shapes within the quilt, and brings the viewer's eye back into the main design of the quilt. Entirely apart from the practical matter of enlarging the quilt to fit a particular space or bed, a border provides an area to add another element to the quilt as well as to enhance its overall design.

Pieced borders are the elite of "borderdom," and they can take a quilt from nice to noteworthy, but they are made less often than plain fabric borders. The difficulty of designing a pieced border and making it fit the quilt (and the penchant for stretching inherent in a pieced border) discourages many quilters and leads them to settle on a single-fabric frame for the quilt.

We urge you not to give up on the chance to add another dimension to your quilt. Foundations will solve the stretching problem and will make sure you end up with the size you planned. Stability, so important in block piecing for accuracy, is doubly so for long strips of piecing, which can "grow" several inches even with careful handling.

Both simple and intricate borders can be designed and drawn directly on foundations. Making notations of color, fabric placement, and piecing sequence right on the foundation is an enormous help in avoiding the frustration of mispositioned fabrics. The same techniques quilters are familiar with for block foundation piecing are used for stitching a foundation border. In fact, you may become emboldened to construct multiple pieced borders, knowing that they will fit perfectly. Smoother piecing, no stretching – what more could a quilter want?

There is the phenomenon of math anxiety that some claim prevents them from making pieced borders fit and flow around the corners. Frankly, we think this problem is over-rated. Nobody is born knowing how to quilt, but we learn. Math literacy is just another learning process, and because so much of quiltmaking is involved with mathematics, it is a skill you have probably already unconsciously absorbed as you learned to quilt. If you think you haven't, we'll help by showing you ways to make your border fit your quilt without undue pain and suffering.

Our aim is to show you both simple and more complex approaches to pieced borders, as well as some of the finer points of piecing borders on foundations. We hope you will be inspired to explore ways to make your next quilts even more exciting.

CHAPTER 1
Border Design

Although many antique quilts did not have borders and many contemporary art quilts are made with small or no frames, most quilts are improved by a well thought-out border. There is no one best answer, but if you take some time to study your quilt and consider the possibilities, you will likely gain some insight into what would be appropriate as a frame.

There are times when the border almost designs itself. At others, the possibilities are so many as to be incapacitating. We think that one reason there are so many single-fabric borders is because they provide by far the simplest and quickest way to end a quilt. But given what we know about design and the effect of pieced borders, coupled with the use of foundations, there is no longer any need to take the quick and easy route.

The most important tool you have is your eye. You can train yourself to find the proportion and scale that will fit a quilt top, to see shapes within your quilt that can be a focus for a border design, and to detect the relationship of color values that will shape the design, perhaps adding depth and shading. To start thinking about what would best enhance your quilt, you can ask yourself some questions about the quilt itself.

DESIGN QUESTIONS

What style is your quilt? Is it traditional, country, folk, classic, or innovative? Each creates a special mood that you may want to accentuate with the border design. The technique used for the quilt top is usually less of a consideration than the style of the quilt. Look first within your quilt for geometric shapes, segments of blocks, or parts of the design that would complement the quilt. Pieced borders can be combined with appliqué quilts and can even be used with appliqué elements or with another appliqué border.

The border does not necessarily even have to repeat elements in the quilt. The border for Dixie's quilt (Photo 1–1, page 8) is one of many in which the border has the colors and fabrics of the quilt, but not the shapes. Dixie used an innovative coloration of the pieced pineapple block to border Hawaiian appliqué pineapple motifs, but you don't have to understand this whimsical connection to see that the border design is eminently suited to the quilt.

Another appropriate border that does not repeat shapes but ties in directly with the theme of the quilt is found in Laurie Berdahl's NAUTICAL JOURNEYS AND DOLPHIN DREAMS (Photo 1–2). The swirling Snail's Trail blocks in the border simulate ocean waves surrounding the bevy of boats and dolphins.

Are you making a specific size? Does it need to fit a particular bed or wall space? What size are the blocks or design elements within the quilt? Do you want sashing or inner borders? They can be both a size extender and a design element, and ideally, should be configured in your original plans.

Is the border proportionate? Proportion is as important as the design itself. A too-narrow border looks trivial. A too-wide one overpowers the body of the quilt and is a case of the tail wagging the

PHOTO 1–1. Border detail for UNTITLED, by Dixie Haywood. Full quilt shown on page 9. PHOTO: MELLISA KARLIN MAHONEY

PHOTO 1–2. Border detail for NAUTICAL JOURNEYS AND DOLPHIN DREAMS, by Laurie Berdahl. Full quilt top shown on page 9.

PHOTO 1–3. Border detail for NEBULA, by Jane Hall. Full quilt shown on page 9.

dog. You may need to adjust the size and number of blocks to make the proportion work.

There are no cut-and-dried rules for figuring the width of a border. It has been said that the border "should" be at least the size of a block from the quilt. Sashes "should" be approximately one-fourth the block size. These are not absolutes. The relationship of fabric to design is different for every quilt. Use the size "rules" as starting points, then suit yourself as to size and proportion.

The best design tool you can have for determining border width is a design wall. If you don't have one, you can simply pin the quilt top to a wall or drape it over the couch, leaving it there to study it. Your eye will eventually tell you what looks right. If your eye goes to the border first, it may not be the right one for the quilt. A good border can make a quilt, but it cannot save a bad quilt.

How many borders will be used? Proportion also relates to the number of borders and their relationship to each other. Many border designs work well in multiples, either as mirror images or as multiple sizes of a design. You may need one or two single-fabric borders between the body of the quilt and the pieced border, either to give some breathing room or to achieve a needed measurement so the pieced border will fit exactly. It is often desirable to add a final single-fabric border to enclose the pieced border and, not so incidentally, to make the squaring up of the finished quilt easier. The width of all the borders together, not just individually, should be a factor in your planning.

Which colors are dominant? The colors in the border can accentuate or contrast with the color scheme of the quilt, but they will affect it. For instance, bordering a scrap quilt in one or two colors used in the quilt body will make those colors "pop." Using all the colors of the quilt in the border will mellow the total effect. It depends on the look you want. Jane's NEBULA (Photo 1–3) has three thin inner borders, one each of three bright colors used in the interior of the quilt. She tried one border, then two, and realized it was necessary to use all

UNTITLED, 62" x 62", by Dixie Haywood. PHOTO: MELLISA KARLIN MAHONEY

NAUTICAL JOURNEYS AND DOLPHIN DREAMS, quilt top, 70" x 90", by Laurie Berdahl. Clipper ship patterns by Stephanie Martin Glennon.

NEBULA, 58" x 58", by Jane Hall.

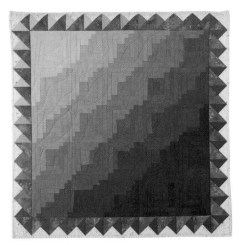

PARADISE, 30" x 30", by Jane Hall.

GEESE TRAILS, 24" x 24", by Jane Hall. PHOTO: MELLISA KARLIN MAHONEY

TRIBUTE TO THE MERCHANTS' MALL, 62" x 98", by Eileen Sullivan.

three to make the best color frame. The wide navy outer border helps declare that this is a blue quilt.

Quilters are frequently taught to use only the fabrics and colors from within the quilt body for the border rather than introducing new ones. This might be true when just a few fabrics are used in a quilt, or if it has a single-fabric border, but we think this dictum can be relaxed with pieced borders. It is often possible to use a fabric in the border that is similar in color to one used in the quilt body without creating a major visual discontinuity. Jane pieced PARADISE (Photo 1–4) with a packet of hand-dyed fabrics and did not have enough leftover pieces to make a border. She found a subtle print that incorporated some of the original colors and was able to combine it with small scraps of the original fabrics to make a successful pieced border.

Pairing pieced and plain borders is often a good ploy. A pieced border doesn't necessarily have to be the only border or have to be on the outside of the quilt. Using strips of plain fabric next to the quilt creates a transition from the interior piecing and helps emphasize the piecing in the border, as in Jane's GEESE TRAILS (Photo 1–5). Single strips of fabric are also sometimes essential to make the pieced border fit the edge of the quilt. Apart from the technical aspects however, an interior pieced border can be an extremely effective design.

Will the blocks and border be integrated? Designs from the quilt – whole blocks, partial blocks, or elements from any design within the quilt – can be extended into the border, providing a unique transition to the outside edge of the quilt or subsequent borders. Eileen Sullivan's TRIBUTE TO THE MERCHANTS' MALL quilt (Photo 1–6) is a simple example of such a border on a traditional design.

In some quilts, such as CALIFORNIA REEL (Photo 1–7, full quilt shown on page 105), Allison Lockwood's innovative version of the Virginia Reel block, the borders meld with the quilt so well that it's difficult to determine where the quilt design ends and the border begins. Color is the clue to the transition, effectively countering convention with a

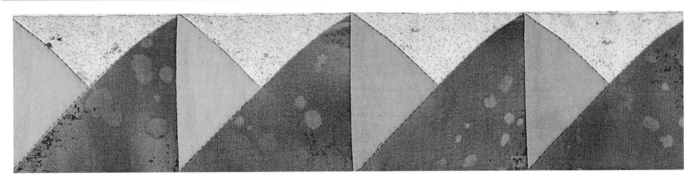

PHOTO 1–4. Border detail for PARADISE, by Jane Hall. Full quilt shown on page 10.

PHOTO 1–5. Border detail for GEESE TRAILS, by Jane Hall. Full quilt shown on page 10. PHOTO: MELLISA KARLIN MAHONEY

PHOTO 1–6. Border detail for TRIBUTE TO THE MERCHANTS' MALL, by Eileen Sullivan. Full quilt shown on page 10.

PHOTO 1–7. Border detail for CALIFORNIA REEL, by Allison Lockwood. Full quilt shown on page 105.

PHOTO 1–8. Border detail for TWENTIETH CENTURY SILKIE, by Claudia Clark Myers. Full quilt shown on page 101.

PHOTO 1–9. Border detail for HOT COTTON, by Dixie Haywood. Full quilt shown on page 74.

lighter edge to the quilt. Claudia Clark Myers' TWENTIETH CENTURY SILKIE (Photo 1–8) is composed of a series of borders, with the final one relating the edge of the quilt to the center, more with color than with shape.

Pieced sashing can also be used to integrate a border with a quilt. In HOT COTTON (Photo 1–9), Dixie connects the appliqué blocks with pieced sashing, which is repeated in the border. The diamonds used in both are the same size, with those in the sashing placed horizontally and those in the border aligned vertically. This arrangement creates a proportional difference between the width of the sashing and the border while retaining a visual connection.

In the best of all possible worlds, we would plan the border at the time we plan the body of the quilt. This method makes it possible to make adjustments in block size and quilt size, if needed, to work out the design to best advantage and to know what comes next. Alas, here in the real world, we often change our ideas as the quilt proceeds, throwing our best-laid plans aside as we become more intimately connected with the quilt. Even with the best computer program and personal design skills, there is nothing like seeing the quilt in the cloth. While planning your entire quilt before you start can provide peace of mind, do not let a plan keep you from mid-course changes. Remember that originality is often just a creative response to a problem.

CORNERS

Once a border design has been chosen, the sticking point for many quilters is turning the corner in a logical and pleasing way. Some designs wrap around a corner easily, some require especially creative thinking, and a few present insurmountable problems. A block or design from the interior of the quilt often makes a good corner insert, providing continuity and balance.

Borders composed of squares or triangles are the easiest shapes from which to work out corner turns. Diamonds can be among the most difficult. Sometimes the best solution is to use a plain corner square, which can be more honest than a contrived solution that trivializes the design. Following through later with quilting designs can tie the plain square to the quilt.

One successful design strategy for borders composed of right-angle triangles is to change direction in the center of the border. Shapes approaching the corners will be mirror images, leading to a variety of possibilities. A particularly elegant corner is seen in Debra Ballard's JOHN'S MICHIGAN MEMORIES (Photo 1–10, page 14), a pieced and appliquéd quilt with two borders of elongated sawtooth triangles. Debra changed directions in the center of her borders but left a large square in each corner in which she echoed a simpler version of her center motif.

Corners can often be included as part of the border foundations. They can be added to one end of each foundation or to both ends of two of them. If this is not possible or desirable, make separate foundations for the corners and join them to the borders after the piecing is completed.

PREPARING FOR BORDERS

After your quilt top is complete, the process for preparing it for borders is the same for both single-fabric and pieced borders. Do a final pressing, making sure all seam allowances are flat and going in the direction you have chosen. Then measure, measure, measure! If you have pieced a top made of 8" blocks and you know that, mathematically, your quilt should measure 64" x 64", measure it carefully to make sure that the measurement is correct. Even with careful piecing and pressing,

CALIFORNIA REEL, corner detail, by Allison Lockwood.

TWENTIETH CENTURY SILKIE, detail, by Claudia Clark Myers.

HOT COTTON, sashing detail, by Dixie Haywood.

PHOTO 1–10. Border detail for JOHN'S MICHIGAN MEMORIES, by Debra Ballard. Full quilt shown on page 67.

JOHN'S MICHIGAN MEMORIES, corner detail, by Debra Ballard.

you may find that it has grown or shrunk as much as an inch. Fabric is fickle and seam allowances may not all be exact, so there may need to be some adjustments in the border to accommodate the actual measurements of the quilt body.

Measure horizontally and vertically across the middle of the quilt along a stabilized seam to find the true width and length for the borders. Then compare the outer edge measurements to the center ones. Make sure that the opposite sides are the same measurement. Also measure both diagonals across the quilt. If they are the same, then the quilt is straight.

Even if the sides of the quilt are on-grain, the unstitched edges can stretch. It is good insurance to stay-stitch the edges within the seam allowance. You can ease the edges slightly, as you stay stitch, to ensure that they measure the same as the centers. Any discrepancies need to be corrected at this point, even if you need to restitch certain areas. They do not correct themselves and will infect subsequent borders like an out-of-control virus.

If you are adding a single-fabric border, mark and cut it to the correct measurement before attaching it, rather than adding a too-long strip of fabric and trimming it afterward. This method will help maintain the correct size, but repeat the squaring-up process each time a border is added, whether it is single-fabric or pieced.

BORDER MATH

Quilters use math constantly, whether they are consciously aware of it or not. The simplest borders, whether single-fabric or pieced, require only measurements derived from the lengths of the sides of the quilt. When you are working with borders containing repeated shapes, math becomes more of a factor.

The first and most basic calculation for the next level of pieced border is to determine the grid of one piecing unit, both its length and height. If you are using blocks or partial blocks from the quilt for the border, the unit grid will be the same as that of the block, so it will be an easy fit. The easiest way to fit a border with pieced units is to make sure the unit size is a division of the block size so the border will fit the quilt top without mathematical gymnastics.

For example, 8" blocks can be divided to accommodate 1", 2", and 4" units. Nine-inch blocks will divide easily into 1", 1½", and 3" units. Twelve-inch blocks offer units of 1", 1½", 2", 3", 4", and 6". Sashing the same width as your border unit will, of course, be the easiest to work with. If you want to insert a framing border between the quilt top and the pieced border, pick a measurement that is either half the unit size or some other easily measured division of the unit. Keeping all the measurements compatible is the simplest way to work.

Units that relate to the block size are not always possible or even preferable. Diagonal sets, a combination of asymmetric blocks in the quilt top, and shapes or designs that don't divide evenly require dealing with the total dimension of the quilt top to find a suitable unit size. Try dividing your border measurements into twos, threes, fours, or fives to find a unit size that will fit evenly.

A rectangular quilt top may complicate the process of finding a common denominator for all sides. You can use a calculator to work out a division or resort to that oldest quilt trick – folding and refolding a strip of paper the size of the border until you find the perfect unit size. If you have a computer and a quilt design program, much of this figuring can be done automatically as you explore various options.

Single-fabric borders can have more than an aesthetic appeal. They often play a valuable part in making the math work. When used for this purpose, they are called "spacers." For instance, if you need three more inches for a unit to fit, adding 1½" spacers on each side will solve the problem. For rectangular quilts, it is not uncommon to need spacers of different widths for the vertical and horizontal strips, for instance, 3" for the length and 4" for the width. In this case, two parallel sides would have 1½" spacers, and the other two sides would have 2" spacers. When the quilt is complete, the half-inch difference will be visually negligible. The important thing is that the pieced units are even and flow smoothly and that the corner treatments are integrated with the border design.

When planning pieced borders, if the discrepancy in measurements is small enough, another possible solution is to use the "fudge factor." For instance, you may want to use 2" units but are left with a 1¾" remainder. Fudge by shaving a thread's width off of evenly spaced units. Conversely, you could widen units by a thread or two to use up a small difference without having to add another unit and upset the mathematical calculations. The variance will never be noticed. This sort of adjustment may be useful when you can't arrive at a common measurement on borders for both the length and width of the quilt. These adjustments are easily made when marking the foundations, leaving nothing to chance as the piecing proceeds.

Mathematics for borders can be simple, and once the basics are understood, adjustments are much easier to calculate. We will detail some of these in the chapters relating to different shapes and designs.

CHAPTER 2
Using Foundations

While using a foundation for precise piecing and for designing is invaluable for any design, we consider that its use as a stabilizer is essential for piecing borders, because of their length. The choice of foundation materials for borders is basically the same as for any foundation piecing. Permanent foundations, such as fabric or interfacing, will remain in the quilt. Temporary foundations include papers of various sorts as well as tear-away interfacing. We prefer light-weight foundations of whatever material is used, to avoid distorting the stitching when the foundations are removed.

All materials offer stability at various levels, but for borders, we narrow the choices down considerably. You need a foundation material that can be cut into long strips and one that is relatively durable because the piecing includes so many short seams.

MATERIALS AND MARKING
FREEZER PAPER

We frequently use freezer paper for borders. It adheres to the fabric pieces and will not stretch. It is particularly appropriate for borders with points or many small pieces. Unlike pieced blocks, in which each patch is often stitched on several sides, borders have a more limited seam stabilization because many border patches are stitched on only one or two sides. The added grip of freezer paper provides insurance that the pieces will be held in place.

The pattern can be traced on freezer paper, as with all foundations. However, freezer paper can easily be needle-punched, making it possible to mark many foundations at one time. To needle punch multiple foundations, pin a traced pattern section on top of a stack of freezer-paper strips and machine stitch on all the lines with an unthreaded needle to perforate the layers. When you have finished, check from the bottom of the stack to make sure you have "sewn" all the lines before removing the marked pattern. (Freezer paper with graph lines is useful for marking the top foundation section, ensuring an extra measure of precision.)

To help maintain control as you needle punch, lay a piece of muslin under the freezer-paper stack as a buffer between the slippery paper and the feed dogs. It is important, when stitching multiple layers, that you position each foundation piece with the same side down. If you neglect this detail, you will create mismatched as well as mirror-imaged borders, which can be a problem if you are dealing with directional designs. However, when mirror-imaged sections are needed, freezer paper can be alternately layered by folding it accordion-style before needle punching it.

Lengths of borders can be needle punched together at one time, so you will need to draw the border only once. Alternatively, to eliminate the necessity of drawing the entire border, a stack of short sections can be marked by needle-punching. When the border can be pieced as one continuous strip, it is convenient to start piecing on one short section of freezer paper, then add the next section, when needed, by overlapping the two pieces of the freezer paper and ironing them together. You can roll or fold the sections, pinning or paper-clipping them to keep the sections out of the way as you sew.

INTERFACING

Lightweight removable interfacing can do dual duty as either a permanent or temporary border foundation. It is washable, and if left in the quilt, it is lightweight enough to allow comfortable hand quilting while providing enough substance to make a wall quilt hang well. The designs must be drawn individually because needle punching will not be visible on this surface.

Interfacing is more flexible to work with than freezer paper, and it does not tear prematurely at the seam lines as paper can. It can also be used with an ink-jet computer printer to mark designs, but tracing is more practical for marking long borders. Fabric does not adhere to interfacing as it does to freezer paper, so floppy edges need to be secured to the foundation with basting stitches after piecing.

TRACING PAPER AND FABRIC

Tracing paper, a favorite of ours for block piecing, generally does not do as well for a long border foundation because it is more fragile. We detail where it might be suitable, when discussing individual patterns. A fabric foundation is viable for a quilt that will be machine quilted because it adds permanent stability. When using any permanent foundation, you may want to include the seam allowance in the foundation for a sturdier seam.

The extended length of a border calls for careful tracing of the pattern. Use a sharp pencil and off-set the ruler slightly so the pencil recreates the original line exactly. Special care should be taken to avoid "pattern creep" across the lines, caused by cumulative inaccuracies. It is a good idea to begin drawing pattern lines in the middle of the border and work toward each end. If any slight inaccuracies develop as you progress, it is an easy matter to correct them.

PHOTOCOPIES

We strongly advise against photocopying. Even the best copy machine will sometimes distort your pattern, which effectively cancels precision. In addition, the weight of copy paper is a drawback.

PREPARING FOUNDATIONS

Foundations can be made the finished size of the borders. They can also be made with ¼" seam allowances included around the edges. Either way, after the piecing is completed, the fabric edges must be stabilized by stitching inside the seam allowance. While it is easier to stay-stitch if the seam allowance has been included in the foundations, picking out ¼" bits of foundation redefines the meaning of "dog work." We prefer making foundations without seam allowances to avoid this problem. The following tips will help you prepare your foundations.

○ Cut four foundations the length and width of the finished borders. Depending on the border design, the foundations can be made whole or in segments that are joined after piecing. Strips sets can also be sewn on foundations and the slices resewn to complete a border design.

○ If butted corners can be included in the border piecing, add them at the end of two of the border foundations. For mitered corners, add the angled corner to each end of all four foundations. When separate corner pieces are needed, prepare a foundation for each corner.

○ If you are piecing the border in segments, cut the lengths apart after making notations on the foundation indicating the top of the piece, the piecing order, and the color choices. It is also possible to draw, print, or needle punch groups of segments individually.

PIECING

STITCH LENGTH

The foundation material being used will determine the stitch length needed. A normal stitch length is suitable for a permanent foundation. Adjust to a shorter stitch length for a temporary foundation to avoid distortion and loose stitches when the foundations are removed.

We recommend using 14 to 16 stitches to the inch if you have a domestic sewing machine or the 1.50 to 1.75 setting on a metric machine. This shorter stitch length should also be used when piecing on freezer paper. This length will secure the fabrics during removal of the foundations and will still be long enough for ordinary mortals to "unsew," if necessary.

There is no need to backstitch when sewing on foundations. Simply begin and end the line of stitching with two to three extra stitches beyond the ends of the lines. Succeeding lines of sewing will cross the stitches and anchor them in place.

TECHNIQUES

Random top pressed-piecing

The basic technique we use for foundation piecing is pressed-piecing, commonly called "flip and sew." In many of the string and crazy-quilt designs, in which there is no need to match lines or points, we use what we call *random top* pressed-piecing, which involves stitching on top of an unmarked foundation.

1. Position a piece of fabric right side up on the foundation and pin it in place. Be sure the patch extends at least ¼" beyond the foundation at the outer edges (Figure 2–1).

2. Lay a second piece of fabric on top of the first, with right-sides together, matching the cut edges of the fabrics along the side to be sewn. Stitch through all layers with a ¼" seam allowance (Figure 2–2).

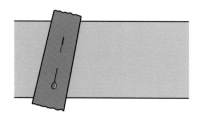

FIGURE 2–1. First piece pinned in place on top of an unmarked foundation.

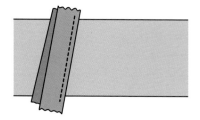

FIGURE 2–2. Second piece added and sewn.

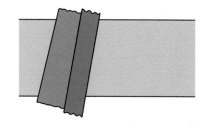

FIGURE 2–3. Second piece of fabric pressed open.

3. Press open the second piece of fabric and pin in place. (Figure 2–3).

4. Continue adding pieces of fabric until the foundation is covered.

Precise top pressed-piecing

In some designs, we use *precise top* pressed-piecing on a marked foundation. The pattern lines are for fabric placement rather than sewing. The foundation is sewn with the drawn side up.

1. Draw the pattern, to which fabric placement lines have been added, on the foundation.

2. Cut the fabric patches with exact ¼" seam allowances.

3. Position and pin a piece of fabric on the marked side of the foundation, right side up. It should fit exactly inside the fabric placement lines (Figure 2–4).

4. Place the second patch on top of the first, with right sides together and cut edges aligned. Sew exactly ¼" from the fabric placement line (Figure 2–5). An accurate seam allowance width is the key to precision.

5. Open the second piece of fabric and press it against the foundation. Its cut edge should just meet but not cover the next fabric placement line (Figure 2–6). Trim if necessary and pin in place.

6. Continue adding pieces of fabric until the foundation is covered.

Under pressed-piecing

For most patterns, we prefer *under* pressed-piecing, in which stitching lines are drawn on the foundation. While this technique may be confusing initially, it is quickly mastered. It does not

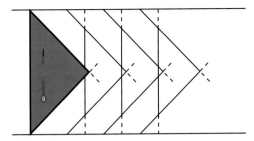

FIGURE **2–4.** First piece of fabric pinned in place.

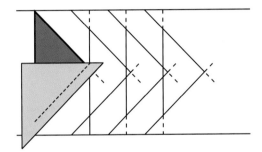

FIGURE **2–5.** Second piece of fabric added and sewn.

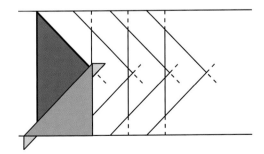

FIGURE **2–6.** Second patch pressed open.

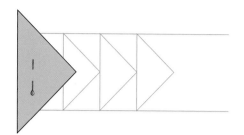

FIGURE 2–7. First fabric piece pinned on undrawn side of foundation.

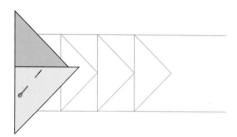

FIGURE 2–8. Second piece of fabric pinned in place.

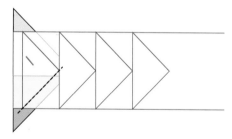

FIGURE 2–9. Sewing on the drawn line, with the fabric against the feed dogs.

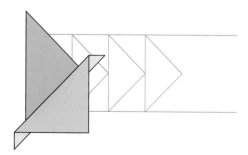

FIGURE 2–10. Second piece pressed open and pinned.

depend on the ability of the stitcher to maintain an accurate ¼" seam allowance, and it results in extremely accurate piecing. Once you are accustomed to sewing upside-down, it becomes almost second-nature.

1. Draw the pattern on a foundation.

2. With the drawn side of the foundation facing downward, position the first piece of fabric right side up on the undrawn side of the foundation. Be sure the patch extends at least ¼", but not more, beyond the first sewing lines (Figure 2–7).

3. Lay a second piece of fabric on top of the first with right sides together. Align the edges to be sewn. Pin through all layers, making sure the pin is placed well away from the stitching line (Figure 2–8).

4. Turn the foundation over so the fabric is against the feed dogs and the foundation is on top. Sew on the drawn line, beginning and ending two stitches at both ends of the line (Figure 2–9).

5. Open the second piece of fabric, press it against the foundation, and pin it in place (Figure 2–10).

6. After each addition, with the drawn side facing up, fold the foundation back along the next sewing line. Trim any excess seam allowance to a scant ¼" beyond the fold (Figure 2–11). This step is important because it provides an accurate edge against which to lay the next piece of fabric.

7. Continue adding pieces of fabric until the foundation is covered.

SINGLE FOUNDATION PIECING

We have included *single* foundation piecing as a foundation method. It is not as commonly used as pressed-piecing, but we believe it is a valid foundation technique because a foundation is used to provide stability and precision. It is an updated version of English template piecing, but instead of the patches being basted and whip-stitched, they are hand or machine sewn together by using the edges of the templates as guides.

In this technique, a finished-sized, freezer-paper template is pressed on the wrong side of the fabric, and the shape is cut with a ¼" seam allowance on all sides. The patch can be sewn to press-pieced units or other single patches, providing precision and allowing all parts of the pieced pattern to be the same weight. This method has application for some border designs.

FABRIC CUTTING

Pressed-piecing, with the fabric folded against the extra layer of the foundation, requires a little more fabric than conventional piecing. Cutting fabric pieces for under pressed-piecing sightly larger than for conventional piecing builds in goof-proofing for minor adjustments and ensures that your patch will cover the next stitching line even if the piece is slightly mispositioned. Cut patches with a ⅜" seam allowance rather than ¼" to save time and aggravation. The only exception to the larger cut is the first piece laid down on a foundation. It should have an accurate ¼" seam allowance to properly position the next piece.

You can use established quick-cutting techniques, adjusted with the extra seam allowance, for cutting right-angle triangles. To make these oversized half-square triangles, cut a square with sides 1¼" longer than the short side of the finished-sized triangle. Then cut the square apart on the diagonal to make two triangles (Figure 2–12a). For quarter-square triangles, cut a square with sides measuring 1¾" more than the long side of the finished-sized triangle. Cut the square on both diagonals to create four triangles (Figure 2–12b). There are a variety of printed papers available for piecing triangles singly or in rows (see Resources, pages 124 and 125).

To cut fabric for any other shape, regular or asymmetrical, make rough-cut templates of scrap or

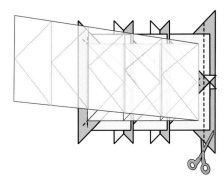

FIGURE 2–11. Foundation folded back, with seam allowance ready for trimming to a scant ¼".

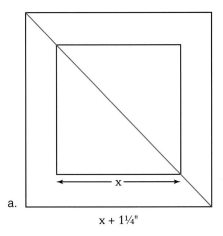

a.

x + 1¼"

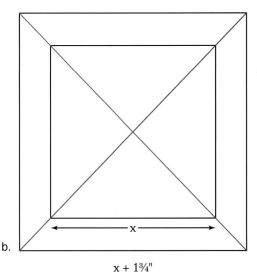

b.

x + 1¾"

FIGURE 2–12. (a) Cutting half-square triangles. (b) Cutting quarter-square triangles.

Figure 2–13. Example of a finished-sized, rough-cut template on a fabric piece.

freezer paper and use them as guides to add ⅜" seam allowances to the fabric pieces. These finished-sized templates allow you to maintain proper fabric print or grain lines as well as to ensure having ample-sized patches (Figure 2–13). This extra step is a small price to pay for the speed and luxury of having the pieces amply cover the space. Trimming excess fabric from the seam allowances after each line is stitched is vital to produce an accurate edge against which to place the next piece to be sewn. Trimming also reduces bulk and makes it easier to quilt across seams.

PRESSING AND TRIMMING

Pressing is important at every step of the way. Press firmly against the previous seam from the fabric side as each piece is added, checking to see that no pleat has been pressed in before sewing the next seam. When the border is complete, press well on both sides before trimming any excess seam allowances around the edges. Remember to avoid touching the shiny side of the freezer paper with the iron.

No matter which pressed-piecing technique you are using, after the foundation has been covered with patches, trim the fabric that extends beyond the outer edges of the foundation to a ¼" seam allowance. The edge of the foundation is the sewing line for attaching the border to the quilt. If you are using a temporary foundation and this is the final border on the quilt, stay-stitch just inside the seam allowance to prevent stretching when the foundation is removed. If adding subsequent borders, leave the foundation in place until the next border has been sewn.

SEGMENTS

Pressed-piecing, whether from the top or the underside, has a built-in geometric limitation. It is impossible to press-piece a set-in (or Y) seam on a foundation. This limitation can be overcome by cutting the foundation into segments which can be press-pieced, then joining the pieced segments to complete the design. Some borders, mostly string and crazy quilt designs as well as some triangle patterns, can be pieced in their entirety on one long border foundation. Other borders, such as those made with squares, diamonds, or block patterns, may need to be cut into segments that will be joined after piecing. When dealing with a segmented design, it is more efficient and more precise to draw the entire design on a foundation and cut it apart rather than draw individual segments.

REMOVING FOUNDATIONS

Foundations should not be removed until the quilt is ready to layer or until the foundation has been stabilized by the addition of another border. You need the foundation in place to provide a stitching guide and stability for the border. If the foundation border is at the edge of the quilt, in addition to stay-stitching, you can add a preshrunk, narrow twill tape or polyester ribbon to the wrong side of each outside edge. The tape can remain in place permanently.

CHAPTER 3
No-Math and Low-Math Borders

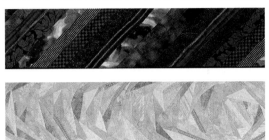

STRING PIECING

Piecing on top of an unmarked foundation is the oldest method of foundation piecing. It has been used for well over 100 years in the Western Hemisphere and for even longer in the Mideast and in Asia. We call this technique random top pressed-piecing (described on page 18). These are the easiest pieced borders of all because they require the fewest calculations and can be sewn on one long, unmarked foundation.

String borders have long been a favorite of quilters because they fit that low-math category and use up a lot of leftover pieces of fabric. A string border also creates a frame for a quilt that is more interesting than a single-fabric border could ever be – all with a minimum of stress. String piecing creates texture, especially when many fabrics with the same colors and values are used. A contrasting but related design can be created when the colors of a quilt's interior are used in the framing. This type of border is appropriate for a wide variety of quilts, even when there is no string piecing in the quilt body.

String borders are commonly pieced with their seam allowances perpendicular to the body of the quilt. The strings can all be cut the same width, cut in random widths, or cut at a slight angle. If you want to have random strings, the only mathematics involved is measuring the width of the border desired and deciding on the approximate width of the strings.

If you cut all the strings the same width, any variation in the seam allowance will cause slight differences in string width. When there are no marked lines to follow, some seams may end up slightly off vertical, but the result will have a casual charm that is appropriate for many quilts.

A measured string border, in which each strip is exactly the same size, will create a consistent texture. The only math needed is to determine the most effective strip width. To ensure precision, draw stitching lines on the foundation and use under pressed-piecing. The choice of random strings on an unmarked foundation or measured strings on a marked foundation depends entirely on the effect you want to achieve.

BIG RED, 28" x 28", by Jane Hall.

AUTUMN GARDEN GLORY, 88" x 90", by Marge Nickels and quilted by Arlene Abernathy.

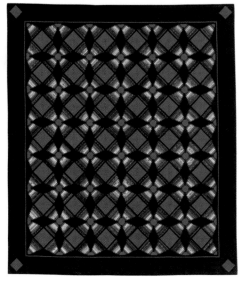

THE ULTIMATE PINEAPPLE, 76" x 87", by Jane Hall.

POINTERS FOR PIECING STRING BORDERS

○ For a random pieced border, because it is difficult to keep the seam lines straight over a long distance, we often draw occasional lines on the foundation, to use as guidelines for positioning the fabric strips.

○ For a measured string border, mark the sewing lines on the foundation. If necessary, add any color notations. Remember, because you are working from the underside, any color progression or asymmetric shape in the finished border will appear as a mirror image relative to the marked side.

○ You can begin at one end of a foundation and piece to the other or start in the center and piece outward toward the ends. The texture that results will depend on the direction in which you piece. If you start in the center, after a few strips have been added, it is possible to chain piece by adding pieces on both sides.

STRING BORDER DESIGNS

String piecing can be used in a variety of formats. In BIG RED (Photo 3–1), Jane used random top pressed-piecing, with straight lines drawn at intervals to use as guidelines. The relatively even, perpendicular string border expands the background for the large single star while adding visual interest with a variety of fabrics similar to the background. The corners were made as separate squares, with the strings fanned out from one corner point (Figure 3–1). The quilting lines in the corners of the body of the quilt echo those fanned lines, multiplying the effect.

Marge Nickels' imaginative curved string border is a wonderful addition to her AUTUMN GARDEN GLORY (Photo 3–2) medallion quilt, showing what a sophisticated effect can be had with this old-fashioned technique. The ribbon of random strings, made of fabrics from the quilt center, was pieced on an unmarked curved foundation. She stay-stitched the turn line and removed the foundation before pressing under the allowances and appliquéing the border to the quilt top. The corner motifs, echoing the center, were appliquéd in place to finish the border. This strong border balances what could have been an overpowering central motif.

In THE ULTIMATE PINEAPPLE (page 24), Jane used low-contrast string piecing, with same-sized strips made of many different shades of black (Photo 3–3). This pieced border does not compete with the focus of the quilt, yet it provides a frame with texture and a subtlety that a single-fabric border could not. The string-pieced corners, repeating a square-on-point shape from inside the quilt, give a stronger finish than a plain corner would have (Figure 3–2).

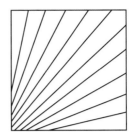

FIGURE 3–1. Corner block for BIG RED.

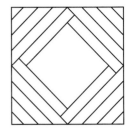

FIGURE 3–2. Corner block for THE ULTIMATE PINEAPPLE.

PHOTO 3–1. Border detail for BIG RED, by Jane Hall. Full quilt shown on page 24.

PHOTO 3–2. Border detail for AUTUMN GARDEN GLORY, by Marge Nickels and quilted by Arlene Abernathy. Full quilt shown on page 24.

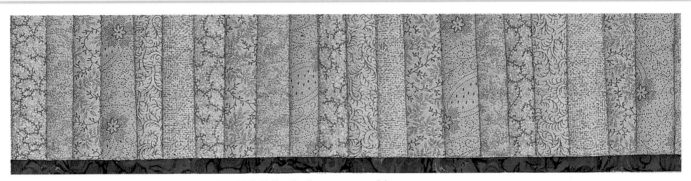

PHOTO 3–3. Border detail for THE ULTIMATE PINEAPPLE, by Jane Hall. Quilt top shown on page 24.

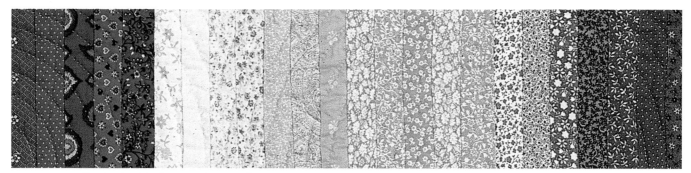

PHOTO 3–4. Border detail for RAINBOW WEAVE, by Dixie Haywood. PHOTO: MELLISA KARLIN MAHONEY

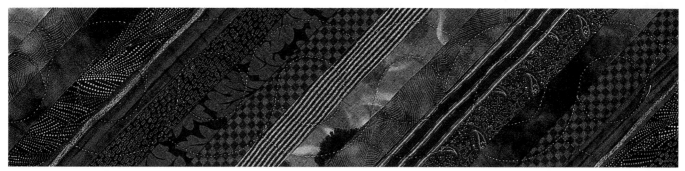

PHOTO 3–5. Border detail for ALTERNATING CURRENT, by Dixie Haywood.

RAINBOW WEAVE, 72" x 72", by Dixie Haywood.
PHOTO: MELLISA KARLIN MAHONEY

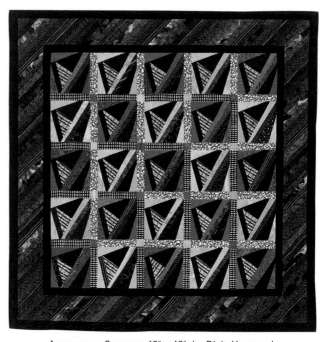

ALTERNATING CURRENT, 49" x 49", by Dixie Haywood.

Dixie used an even-string border in Rainbow Weave (Photo 3–4), which was colored to suggest that the color progression in the quilt was spilling into the border. A corner block was sewn to one end of each border strip, so partial seams were required when the border was attached. To make a partial-seam border like this, sew the first border on, beginning at the left-hand corner of the quilt top and ending 1" or so before the next corner. Leave the 1" section unsewn until the last border has been attached. Working counterclockwise, add the next three borders, beginning each time at a left-hand corner and overlapping the edge of the previously sewn border. After the last border has been attached, complete the seam at the loose end of the first border (Figure 3–3).

The diagonal string border on Dixie's Alternating Current, the latest in her Electric Star series, carries forward the movement of the quilt's diagonal lines with a collection of low-contrast black prints (Photo 3–5). This strong but subtle border visually contains a quilt with vibrant color and complex design detail. To continue the diagonal movement of the strings around the quilt, two corners must be pieced on separate large triangular foundations and added after the borders have been sewn to the quilt (Figure 3–4).

String piecing can be used in infinite variations to create many different graphic effects by tipping the strips at various angles, changing the direction of the angles, and creating compatible corner treatments. The corners can sometimes be pieced on the border foundations, and at other times, they must have separate foundations. In addition to the borders and corner designs shown in Photos 3–4 and 3–5, some common configurations are shown in Figure 3–5, page 28.

CRAZY PIECING

Crazy piecing makes a surprisingly versatile border and is absolutely math-free after the border dimensions have been determined. It is always

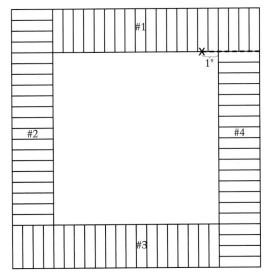

Figure 3–3. Sewing order for the partial-seam border in Rainbow Weave.

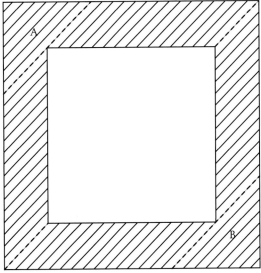

Figure 3–4. Border and corner layout for Alternating Current.

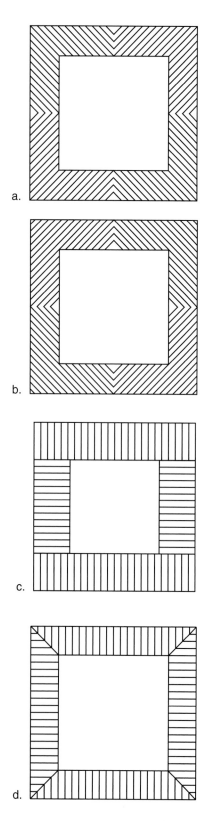

a.

b.

c.

d.

FIGURE 3–5. Angle orientation: (a) inward at mid-border, (b) outward at mid-border, (c) top and bottom borders extend across corners, (d) mitered corners.

OLD GROWTH, 53" x 66", by Dixie Haywood.
PHOTO: MELLISA KARLIN MAHONEY

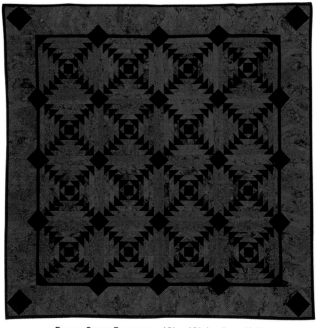

FLYING GEESE PINEAPPLE, 40" x 40", by Jane Hall.

worked on an unmarked foundation by using random top pressed-piecing, described on page 18. In addition, both crazy- and string-pieced borders can be used as final borders without fear that trueing up the edge for the binding will distort any patches or disrupt the design.

Crazy piecing can be embellished when this is compatible with the quilt top, but there are more possibilities if crazy piecing is thought of as a non-embellished design technique to combine fabrics in an unstructured way. There are several color formulas that are especially appropriate for borders.

MULTIPLE PRINTS, SAME COLOR AND VALUE

Use fabrics with a variety of scales and pattern densities. In Dixie's OLD GROWTH (Photo 3–6), the combined effect of the low-contrast yellow fabrics used in the crazy-pieced borders provides a texturally rich border to fit with her concept of sunshine filtering through a forest. The border was pieced on foundations shaped at the ends for mitering. A final green border was pieced with long strips of several green fabrics.

Jane also used this formula in the border for FLYING GEESE PINEAPPLE (Photo 3–7). There are 25 different red prints in the quilt, and they were all used in the crazy-pieced border, making a much more interesting frame than one print could have provided. To complete the on-point squares, she appliquéd triangles where the triangles in the body of the quilt meet the border. The squares extend the block design, spilling it into the border areas. The on-point corner squares, surrounded by string piecing, complete this graphic idea.

PHOTO 3–6. Border detail for OLD GROWTH, by Dixie Haywood. Full quilt shown on page 28. PHOTO: MELLISA KARLIN MAHONEY

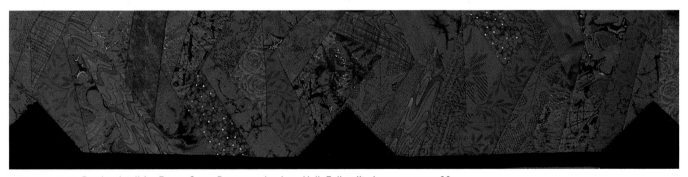

PHOTO 3–7. Border detail for FLYING GEESE PINEAPPLE, by Jane Hall. Full quilt shown on page 28.

Photo 3–8. Border detail for Celebration 2000!, by Dixie Haywood.

Celebration 2000!, 87" x 87", by Dixie Haywood.

Photo 3–9. Crazy Quilt for a Crazy Kid (corner detail), 105" x 105", by Delores Hamilton.

Photo 3–10. Sashing detail for Jewett, Nature at Its Best, by Betty Verhoeven. Full quilt shown on page 31.

SAME COLOR, DIFFERENT VALUES

This approach also has just one color, but with a higher contrast to balance a busier quilt, as seen in Dixie's CELEBRATION 2000! (Photo 3–8) and Delores Hamilton's CRAZY QUILT FOR A CRAZY KID (Photo 3–9).

It often takes trial and error to arrive at a satisfactory border. Dixie's crazy-pieced border for CELEBRATION 2000! was chosen to reinforce the crazy piecing of the circles in the quilt, while highlighting the yellow stars. This solution developed with no small number of adjustments. Trying both a purple and then a yellow crazy-pieced border by themselves on the quilt proved overpowering. Not until the quilt top was tilted and surrounded by the angled border of four different fabrics was the quilt design strong enough for the crazy border. The crazy piecing began in the centers of both the borders and the separately pieced corner squares, creating a circular visual repeat around the edges of the quilt.

For her crazy quilt border, Delores used a lighter palette in the same color but with different values to contrast with the busy blocks of multiple colors and values in her quilt. She comments, "After completing the crazy-pieced blocks, I realized that the cacophony of colors needed visual relief. This led to my decision to create 4" x 6" blocks in icy blues with medium purple triangles for the centers to make a 4" border. That helped set off the brightly colored blocks even more, and yet I found that I needed one more visual break, a solid black 1" inner border."

MULTIPLE COLORS AND VALUES

This combination provides a more traditional crazy-pieced look. It can range from using every color and fabric in a scrap bag, such as Delores used in her quilt, to controlling the palette with a combination of compatible fabrics in selected colors. Using all the colors from a quilt in a crazy-pieced border could give a striking finish, but be aware that this color formula requires finesse to avoid becoming overpowering.

Betty Verhoeven used a softened palette of this formula to create sashing in her JEWETT, NATURE AT ITS BEST history quilt (Photo 3–10), celebrating the 150th anniversary of this Catskill, New York, town. The framed sashing of Victorian-like embellished crazy piecing around each photographic reproduction is both attractive and appropriate to the design of the quilt.

Detail of JEWETT, NATURE AT ITS BEST, by Betty Verhoeven.

JEWETT, NATURE AT ITS BEST, 72" x 78", by Betty Verhoeven.
PHOTO: STU SPERO, CATSKILL MOUNTAIN STUDIO

POINTERS FOR CRAZY-PIECED BORDERS

○ Standard directions for crazy piecing a block can also be used for a border. However, to balance the graphic design, start piecing in the center of the border and work toward each end.

○ A crazy-pieced border, because of its long, narrow shape, requires a variety of cuts to avoid a string look. Use angles and curves to maintain several different sides on which to piece. As you continue to piece, some of the lines formed will grow quite long. To remedy this, sew an ample piece of fabric along the entire line and then make two or more angled cuts, creating a triangle to give shorter lines on which to piece.

○ When you have a choice of two lines on which to add fabric, stitch on the longer line. You cannot solve a long-line problem by piecing on a short adjacent line; this will only lengthen the longer line.

○ Consider the fabric when making cuts. Cutting a long narrow strip along a stripe can reinforce the fabric pattern with the cut. Cutting across a stripe on an angle can add an edgy, vibrant accent.

○ Because the foundation provides stability, you can generally disregard grain lines when making cuts. However, long narrow cuts are easier to sew when they are on grain. If they have been cut along the bias, pin with special care to avoid twisting.

○ The effect of a curve can be achieved without actually making one. Simply stitch two pieces of the same fabric so they cross on either side of a patch, and the eye will see it as a curve.

○ If you are uneasy with the unplanned and unmarked method, initially it may help to draw some placement lines on the foundation. However, it's best not to become dependent on pre-planned crazy piecing. Learn to enjoy designing as you stitch.

Border detail for OLD GROWTH, by Dixie Haywood. Full quilt shown on page 28. PHOTO: MELLISA KARLIN MAHONEY

CHAPTER 4
Strips, Squares and More

The next logical step from simple no-math or low-math borders is a border made with measured shapes. Borders containing specific shapes from within the body of the quilt will not only frame it but also provide continuity with the quilt design.

Most of the simple borders in the previous chapter were constructed on one long border foundation, and they did not require units, divisions, or any math except to determine the total length and width of the border. Measured-shape designs, however, almost always involve calculating the number and size of the units that will fit into the border. If you are lucky, the divisions and the math will fall into place easily. Many times, the sizes of our pieced borders are not what we had planned originally, but they are what will work best, given a particular unit shape and size.

Borders with measured units are best made by pressed-piecing with seam lines marked on a foundation. We usually use under pressed-piecing in which the fabric is positioned under the foundation and the sewing is done on the drawn lines (page 19). It is also possible to use precise top

pressed-piecing, in which the pattern lines are guides for positioning the fabric pieces and you sew with the fabric on top (pages 18–19).

UNITS MADE WITH STRIPS
SIMPLE STRIP DESIGNS

The most simple of the patterned pieced borders contain strips or rectangles. Different from string borders, these designs involve units and slightly more math. As with the string variations, measured strips in designs and units can create diverse and wonderful borders, even with simple colorations.

Strips can be used in measured patterns to create larger squares, triangles, zigzags, or shaded shapes (Photo 4–1, page 34). Some of these designs can be pieced on a whole-border foundation. Others, because of the mechanics of pressed-piecing, will need to be pieced in segments, which are then sewn together to create the border. The strip arrangements shown here are given as patterns on pages 46–50.

PHOTO 4–1. A sampling of strip patterns.

Experiment with the different looks, perhaps pasting up small samples to decide what will work best for your quilt. Pressing strips on a section of freezer paper can provide you with an immediate preview of a possible design. It only takes a short section of the proposed border to give you an idea of the final effect, saving false starts and unnecessary frustration.

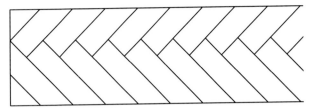

FIGURE 4–1. Woven braid border.

STRIPS IN WOVEN DESIGNS

Strips can be pieced in a woven design to appear as a braid (Figure 4–1). Bonnie Jean Rosenbaum used a variation of a braid in her RAINBOWS IN THE SNOW (Photo 4–2). The alternating strips form a small tight braid, making a good contrast with the curves in the quilt. She pieced the braid with strips of white background fabric, creating a subtle texture that is enhanced by the brightly colored flat piping sewn to each strip. The resulting tiny braid sparkles.

Linda Erickson calls her small quilt TRAILING THE SNAIL. It was pieced with a variety of batik fabrics and has secondary patterns created by the color placement. She created a meandering braided border, with the strips crossing along soft curves rather than on the usual straight line (Photo 4–3, page 36). The border is colored with dark values on the outside, and light fabrics frame the interior in an off-set design. Linda shares the pattern for the border on page 52.

RAINBOWS IN THE SNOW, 42" x 42", by Bonnie Jean Rosenbaum.

PHOTO 4–2. Border detail for RAINBOWS IN THE SNOW, by Bonnie Jean Rosenbaum.

MULTIPLE, LONG STRIPS

Quilters don't often think of piecing narrow borders on a foundation, but it keeps long strips even and straight. Jane had planned to frame NEBULA with an inner border of one of the bright colors in the quilt (Photo 4–4). When she decided more colors were needed, she pieced the long, skinny strips on freezer paper to keep them from wobbling.

In AUSTIN SUNRISE (Photo 4–5), where so much activity is going on in the middle of the quilt with its bright colors and strong graphics, Jane wanted an equally strong border to frame the quilt. One or two borders were not enough, so again, she pieced long strips of varying widths of the two colors on freezer paper for stability.

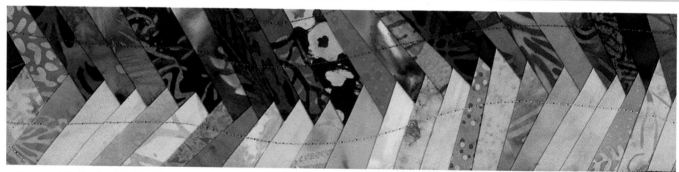

PHOTO 4–3. Border detail for TRAILING THE SNAIL, by Linda J. Erickson. Pattern on page 51. Full quilt shown on page 37.

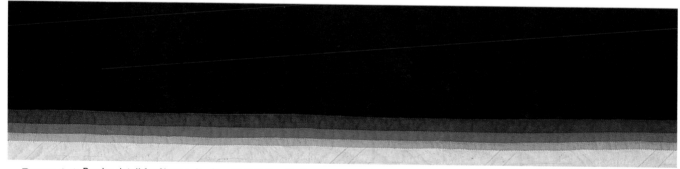

PHOTO 4–4. Border detail for NEBULA, by Jane Hall. Full quilt shown on page 37.

PHOTO 4–5. Border detail for AUSTIN SUNRISE, by Jane Hall. Full quilt shown on page 37.

UNITS MADE WITH SQUARES

Squares in all kinds of designs make popular pieced borders. They can be set straight or on-point, in multiple rows, checkerboards, or woven designs. Sometimes they echo shapes from within the quilt, and sometimes they provide a counterpoint to the quilt design.

CHECKERBOARD SQUARES

The checkerboard border on Dixie's TUITTI-FRUITTI is a case study for the advantages of using foundations to construct borders composed of squares (Photo 4–6, page 38). While foundations were used to piece the quilt blocks, to her everlasting regret, Dixie did not use them for the border. The quilt top measured a true 36". For the border, 24-1½" squares were to fit along each side, with a nine-patch in each corner. After piecing each border, she discovered that it had stretched so much she needed to remove one row on each side to make it fit, leaving 23 squares to a side. While that number worked out visually, the stretching distorted the quilt enough to prevent it from hanging flat. This experience convinced her that even a simple checkerboard design is worth taking the time to mark and sew on foundations.

Another lesson learned from this quilt is the wisdom of a final single-fabric border. It is a rare quilt that does not need to have its edges trimmed to straighten them after quilting and before adding the binding. An outer single-fabric border will keep you from having to cut into the patch shapes when you true up the quilt.

Use the following steps to under press-piece a randomly colored checkerboard border:

1. Draw the full checkerboard for one border on the dull side of a freezer-paper foundation, including the corners. Layer three more sheets of freezer paper, dull sides up, and needlepunch the design. Needlepunching all four borders at once is the most efficient and accurate method for mark-

TRAILING THE SNAIL, 14½" x 14½", by Linda J. Erickson.

NEBULA, 58" x 58", by Jane Hall.

AUSTIN SUNRISE, 78" x 94", by Jane Hall.
FROM THE COLLECTION OF MICHAEL HALL AND LIZ ASTON

PHOTO 4–6. Border detail for TUITTI-FRUITTI, by Dixie Haywood.

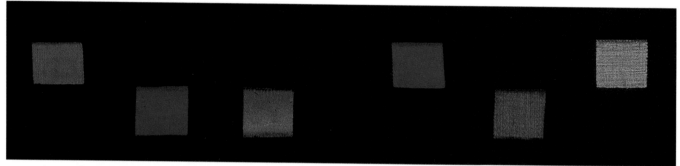

PHOTO 4–7. Border detail for PARTY TIME, by Jane Hall and Dixie Haywood.

TUITTI-FRUITTI, 42" x 42", by Dixie Haywood.

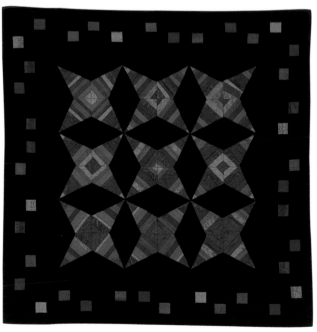

PARTY TIME, 28" x 28", by Jane Hall and Dixie Haywood.

ing the design, but it will create too many corners, so you must cut corners off of two foundations.

2. Mark the checkerboard colors randomly on each foundation. The colors in the finished border will be a mirror image of your marked foundation. On a randomly colored border, this normally won't matter, but if you want it to be exactly as you have marked it, draw with a pencil or permanent fine-line marker on the shiny side of the freezer paper, or reverse your color sequence on the dull side.

3. Label the rows 1, 2, and 3, then cut the foundation apart into three long single rows (Figure 4–2). Press-piece each row, following the under pressed-piecing directions on page 19, until the foundations are covered. So that the seams will fall in opposite directions when the rows are joined, begin the piecing in rows 1 and 3 at the same ends and start piecing row 2 at the opposite end. To avoid mixing up your color arrangement, sew the rows for one border together before you cut the foundation apart for the next border.

4. Sew the short borders to opposite sides of the quilt top and add the long borders with the corner pieces last.

RANDOM SQUARES

PARTY TIME (Photo 4–7) is a small, silk string quilt we made as a collaborative piece. We wanted to "float" confetti-like colored squares of the silk as lively accents in a dark background. The illusion was achieved by an initial 2" border of the background fabric, followed by two different 1" pieced borders of colored squares and background strips, ending with a solid 1" border.

We originally used freezer paper as single foundations (page 20) for the strips of silk. These strips were sewn between the wide strips of navy cotton, which were not attached to freezer paper. The resulting strip-sets were sliced to make the four borders.

UNITS MADE WITH STRIP-SETS
SHORT STRIPS, LONG SLICES

After making PARTY TIME, we rethought the process and have updated the construction with a strip-set foundation technique that is both much easier to piece and more precise. When all the borders are the same size and color, you can join short strips to create a long strip-set, then slice the strip-set lengthwise to create four identical borders that need no further piecing (Figure 4–3).

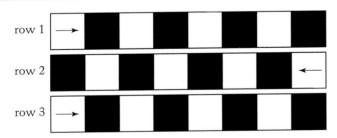

FIGURE 4–2. Checkerboard foundation cut into three single rows.

FIGURE 4–3. Short strips with lengthwise cuts.

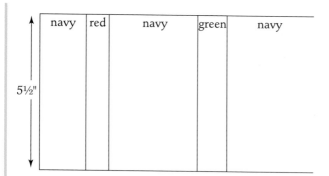

| navy | red | navy | green | navy |

5½"

FIGURE 4–4. Prepared foundation.

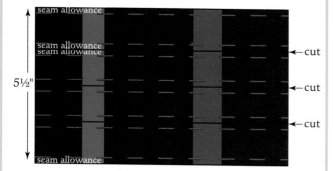

seam allowance
seam allowance
seam allowance
← cut

5½"
← cut

← cut

seam allowance

FIGURE 4–5. Strip-set marked for cutting into four borders.

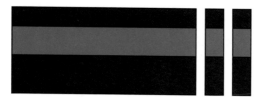

FIGURE 4–6. Long strips with crosswise cuts.

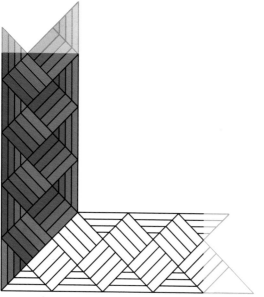

FIGURE 4–7. This four-strand braid is made from two different strip-sets.

The following directions illustrate this vertical strip-set technique, which can be used for any border containing squares or rectangles. The measurements are arbitrary for demonstration purposes. Adjust them to fit your quilt.

1. Cut a piece of freezer paper the finished length of the border and four times the finished width of one of the border strips, plus 1½" to allow for seam allowances. For example, if the border contains four strips that each finish 1", you will need a foundation 5½" wide. If corners are included, add a corner to one end of each foundation. If corners are to be made as separate units, prepare the four corner foundations.

2. Draw the vertical lines on the dull side of the piece of freezer paper and mark the colors of the strips (Figure 4–4). The finished border will be a mirror image of the marked colors.

3. Cut short fabric strips the size of the drawn vertical strips, plus ample seam allowances. Using under pressed-piecing (page 19), stitch each strip in place on the foundation, making sure it extends at least ¼" beyond every side of the foundation. Press and trim the strip before sewing the next one, taking care not to touch the iron to the freezer paper. When the piecing is complete, trim the seam allowance to ¼" beyond all sides of the foundation.

4. To create the four borders, draw four sets of sewing and cutting lines along the length of the border. Notice that each border section must have ¼" seam allowances on all sides. Cut the strip set into four borders (Figure 4–5).

LONG STRIPS, SHORT SLICES

In a more common approach to strip piecing, long strips are sewn together on a foundation. The strip-set is cut into short segments that are joined to create the final design (Figure 4–6). This technique provides absolute accuracy in the sewing of

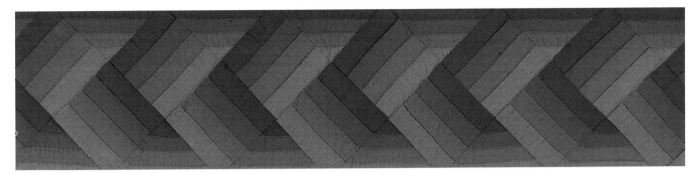

PHOTO 4–8. Border detail for WANDERING FANS, by Brooke Flynn.

the long strips, which makes matching the segments easy. Many designs require making more than one strip-set.

John Flynn is known for his complex braided border patterns, made by using strip-sets without foundations. His wife, Brooke Flynn, used a packet of hand-dyed fabrics to make the border on WANDERING FANS (Photo 4–8). Note how the inner and outer strips form secondary borders. With John's permission, we have adapted one of his workshop designs for foundation piecing (Figure 4–7).

We used two strip-sets on freezer paper, one for the square units and one for the triangle units (Figure 4–8). Both sewing and cutting lines are marked on the foundations before cutting the strip-sets into segments. When the units are joined to make the pattern, the matched seams will be precise, and the lines of color will flow smoothly around the border and corners. Varying the number of strips, using even or odd numbers, will produce vastly different effects.

WANDERING FANS, 40½" x 49½", by Brooke Flynn.

 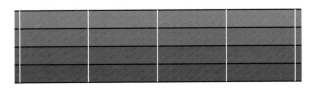

FIGURE 4–8. Braid construction: (a) strip-set for triangles, (b) strip-set for squares.

BARGELLO BORDERS

Strip-sets make it possible to devise designs with even more intricate piecing. The intertwined diagonal rows of squares in the border of WHIRLIGIG enclose the twirling circular motifs in the quilt, repeating the colors and fabrics in a bargello variation (Photo 4–9). The bargello border of THE HOWARD FAMILY QUILT utilizes the major colors of the quilt while surrounding the soft curved appliqué lines with a geometric design that moves

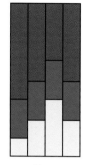

FIGURE 4–9. Four-segment bargello unit.

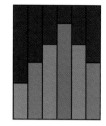

FIGURE 4–10. Six-segment bargello unit.

PHOTO 4–9. Border detail for WHIRLIGIG, by Dixie Haywood. Full quilt shown on page 43. PHOTO: MELLISA KARLIN MAHONEY

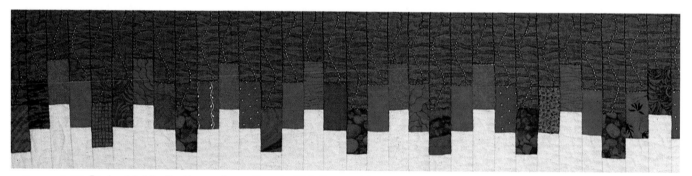

PHOTO 4–10. Border detail for THE HOWARD FAMILY QUILT, by Dixie Haywood. From the collection of Lance and Dana Howard. Full quilt shown on page 43.

PHOTO 4–11. Border detail for SPACE LIGHTS, by Dixie Haywood. Full quilt shown on page 43. PHOTO: MELLISA KARLIN MAHONEY

the eye around the quilt (Photo 4–10). The columnar designs of bargello make an equally good border in SPACE LIGHTS (Photo 4–11). The color progression of hand-dyed fabric was designed to suggest the glow of the aurora borealis.

All three of these borders contain unit arrangements that involve more work with design and mathematics than the previous quilts in this chapter. The border patterns are given on pages 53–56. In both WHIRLIGIG and THE HOWARD FAMILY QUILT, there are four segments to each unit, and two of them are alike (Figure 4–9). In WHIRLIGIG, the duplicate segment is reversed when pieced in the unit, and the color sequence is reversed for every other unit. SPACE LIGHTS has a six-segment unit that contains two sets of duplicates per unit (Figure 4–10).

The corners for bargello quilts need to be planned, because the pattern of "steps" in this design needs to flow around the corner without visual interruption (Figure 4–11). The bargello corners have Log Cabin-type piecing to create the steps. WHIRLIGIG'S corners continue the woven effect of the border design.

WHIRLIGIG, 48" x 48, by Dixie Haywood.
PHOTO: MELLISA KARLIN MAHONEY

THE HOWARD FAMILY QUILT, 108" x 108", by Dixie Haywood.

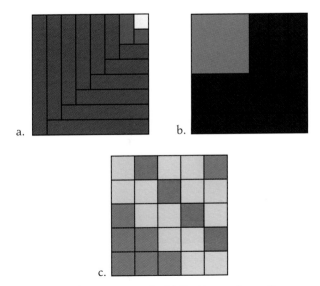

FIGURE 4–11. Corner treatments: (a) THE HOWARD FAMILY QUILT, (b) SPACE LIGHTS, (c) WHIRLIGIG.

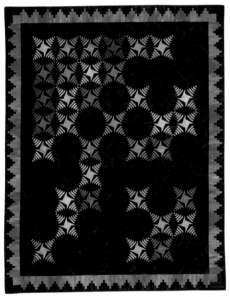
SPACE LIGHTS, 84" x 102", by Dixie Haywood.
PHOTO: MELLISA KARLIN MAHONEY

The next part of the puzzle is how many units to fit along a side. This is a chicken-and-egg question, because the units must be divided into individual cut segments. If there are too few units, the segments may be too wide. If there are too many, they will be too skinny. You may need to play with different combinations to find the most satisfying one. SPACE LIGHTS has ¾" segments, WHIRLIGIG squares measure ⅞", and THE HOWARD FAMILY QUILT segments are 1".

Because the ends of the borders must begin and end at the same step, you will need one extra segment to complete the normal step sequence in WHIRLIGIG and THE HOWARD FAMILY QUILT. In other words, the border for WHIRLIGIG, which has four segments per unit, has 10 units to a side plus one additional segment. In this quilt, the fractional remainder, after the border was divided into 10 units, determined the cut width, making the fit perfect.

The fit for SPACE LIGHTS illustrates the sort of problem solving this type of border may require.

After filling half a page with multiplication and division notations, Dixie solved the problem by reversing the unit at the center of each border, which omits the shortest color segment at that point. She then left out the two shortest segments at all the corners, resulting in four-segment units there (Figure 4–12). The square in the corner block was enlarged to make the correct step-down. This arrangement also made the corner stronger, a serendipitous benefit.

The same design sequence was used for WHIRLIGIG as for the two bargello borders to work out the step sequence and fit. Because it consists of squares rather than strips, it was pieced, like the border for TUITTI-FRUITTI detailed previously, with under pressed-piecing, starting at the same ends for rows 1, 3, and 5, and at the opposite ends for rows 2 and 4. Charts for this border design can be found on pages 53–56.

With all of these types of design that contain squares or strips in predetermined patterns, if you

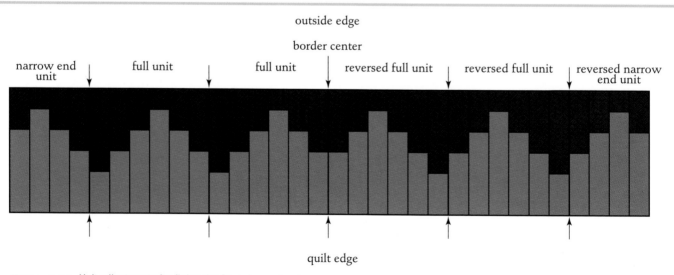

FIGURE 4–12. Unit adjustments for fitting the SPACE LIGHTS border.

piece a segment out of sequence and have pieced beyond it, rip the seam where the error occurred, cut apart the foundation at that point, and add the correct segment. Continue piecing on the joined foundation, adjusting the numbering if needed.

There are three foundation piecing options for this type of border, with advantages and disadvantages to each. Strip-set piecing is used to make the different cut segments for each option, but the time involved, the ease of construction, and the final assembly differ.

❍ In the first method, piece a strip-set on a freezer-paper foundation marked along its length with seam lines for the strips. On the pieced strip-set, mark sewing and cutting lines of the desired width for the segments, then cut the segments. The segments are then pieced together in the pattern sequence. This application works best for larger shapes, such as the John Flynn braid, but can be problematic with narrow bargello segments.

The biggest advantage to this method is that the segments will be precise, and the seams will match perfectly because they were initially stitched on foundations. The disadvantage is that the cut segments, with freezer paper attached, are bulky and not very pliable. The sheer number of segments to be sewn together lends itself to a multiplication of small sewing errors. In addition, removal of the freezer paper from the seam allowances is tedious.

❍ In the second method, piece the strip-set without a foundation by using traditional quick-piecing, that is, sewing strips together along their length with a ¼" seam allowance. The strip-set is then cut into segments, which are pieced together on top of a marked freezer-paper foundation. This method is particularly useful when using narrow segments, and this was the method used for THE HOWARD FAMILY QUILT and SPACE LIGHTS.

The biggest advantage of this method is that the border is a fixed size and will not grow or change with interior stitching. The piecing sequence can be marked on the foundation to avoid any confusion.

The disadvantage of working in this way is that any variation in stitching the original seams of the strip-set will affect the size of the cut segments. Care must be taken in stitching and pressing the seams to avoid distorting the strip-set, and the segments must be cut in exact vertical lines to prevent misalignment of the cut sections when sewing them to the foundation.

❍ The third method combines both of the previous ones. Piece strip-sets on foundations marked with lengthwise sewing lines. Mark the sewing and cutting lines for the segments across the sewn strip-set, then cut the segments apart. Carefully remove the foundations from the segments, and sew them to a finished-size freezer-paper foundation that has been marked with seam lines for the segments.

This technique has the advantages of both the previous methods, with precise cuts and a fixed-size border foundation. Its major disadvantage is that you have to prepare and remove foundations twice. However, the patches in the cut segments are true and can be placed properly with the aid of notations on the border foundation. It is the method Dixie would choose for another bargello border, especially for strip-sets with three or more fabrics.

Simple Strips, Patterns by Jane Hall

FIGURE 4–13. Strips graduated in size and color.

FIGURE 4–14. Shaded strips (pattern on page 48).

FIGURE 4–15. Alternating light and dark strips (pattern on page 48).

FIGURE 4–16. Random-strip fans (pattern on page 49).

DESIGN DETAILS

These simple but effective designs are all pieced by using strips of fabric, and most patterns are sewn on drawn lines. The basic units are easily figured and adjusted to fit a border of almost any length and width. Careful placement of the colors will create zigzags, shaded shapes, and even dimensional effects, all of which form interesting and relatively easy-to-piece borders. Corners can be butted, mitered, or overlapped, or they can be made from separate blocks.

To fit any of these borders to your quilt, find a unit measurement that divides evenly into the border length. Adjust the border width as necessary for good design proportion. We give basic directions for one size of unit.

VERTICAL STRIPS

This design of random-width strips is constructed on a whole-border foundation, rather than in sections (Figure 4–13). It can be sewn with either under or top pressed-piecing, depending on the formality or casualness desired. Graduated colors will create a wave-like line of color, rising and falling around the quilt. No pattern is needed for this design. Mark the foundations with the graduated strip widths, keeping the seams perpendicular to the foundation's edges. Cut fabric strips in varying widths, from ⅜" to 2", plus seam allowances.

SHADED STRIPS

This pattern is constructed on whole-border foundations (Figure 4–14). Draw the basic triangles on long strips of freezer paper, dovetailing the shapes. Mark piecing lines within the triangles depending on the number of shaded stripes desired. The more shades, the more dimensional the unit will appear. Cut fabric strips with ample seam allowances and begin piecing at the end marked #1 by using under pressed-piecing.

ALTERNATING LIGHT AND DARK STRIPS

This design is also pieced on whole-border foundations that have been marked with the basic triangle shapes and piecing lines (Figure 4–15). Use under pressed-piecing. The design will be more successful if you use an even number of strips within each triangle, beginning and ending with a fabric of a different value. The equal amounts of light and dark values will create the illusion of a medium-value border.

RANDOM-STRIP FANS

This design must be pieced in segments, so it is necessary to divide the total border length into square or rectangular units (Figure 4–16). The pat-tern given on page 50 is for 5"-square units sewn with cut fabric strips of varying widths. Using random top pressed-piecing, begin piecing on one of the corner-to-corner diagonals. Stitch subsequent strips, angling them each time to create a fan shape. Piece randomly for best effect. When joining the segments, roughly match the wider ends of the fans to make a flowing line.

DIAGONAL STRIP UNITS

Mark square foundations corner to corner. Then, in one half of the square, mark seam lines parallel to the first line. In the other half, mark lines perpendicular to the first line (Figure 4–17). Note that, if you want to use variation 1, the lines must be spaced identically on each half for the strips to match when the segments are sewn together. For variation 2, it is more interesting to make the widths of the strips different in each half of the segment. Cut fabric strips with ample seam allowances and piece by using under pressed-piecing. Join the segments, setting them side by side or rotating them to create different secondary patterns.

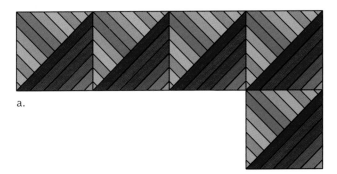

a.

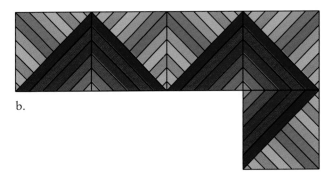

b.

FIGURE 4–17. Diagonal strips: (a) variation 1, (b) variation 2 (pattern on page 50).

4" TRIANGLES

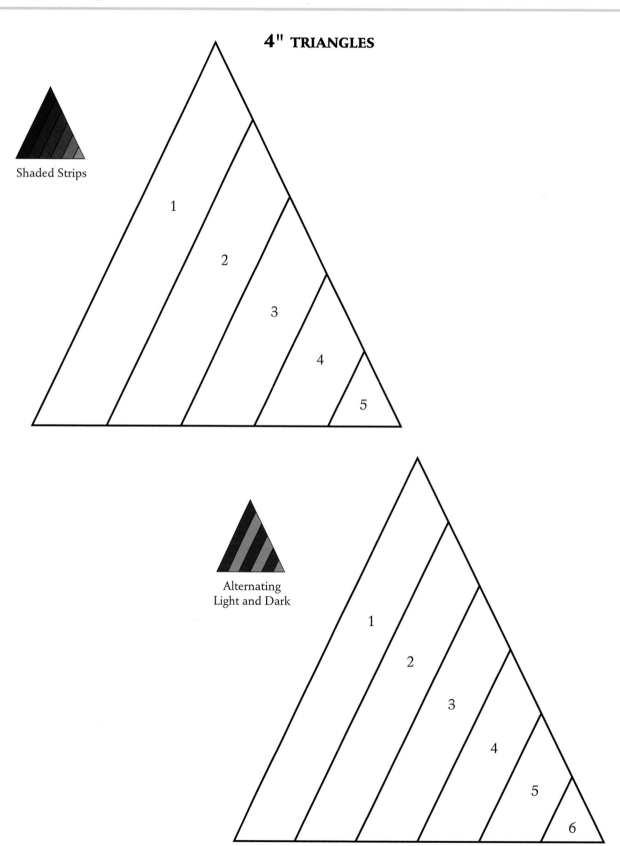

Shaded Strips

Alternating
Light and Dark

5" BLOCK

Random-Strip Fans

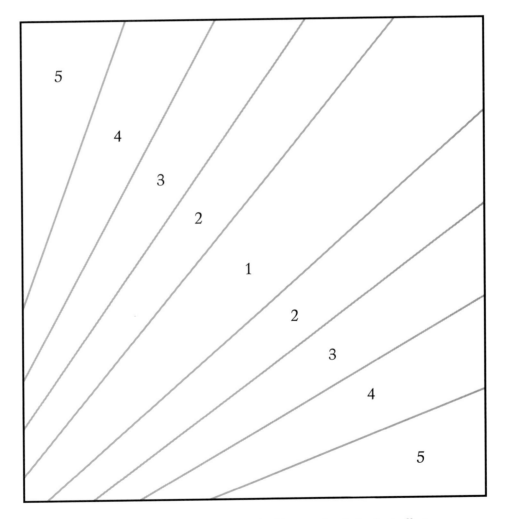

Lines are stitching suggestions only. Piece randomly for best effect.

5" BLOCK

Diagonal Strips

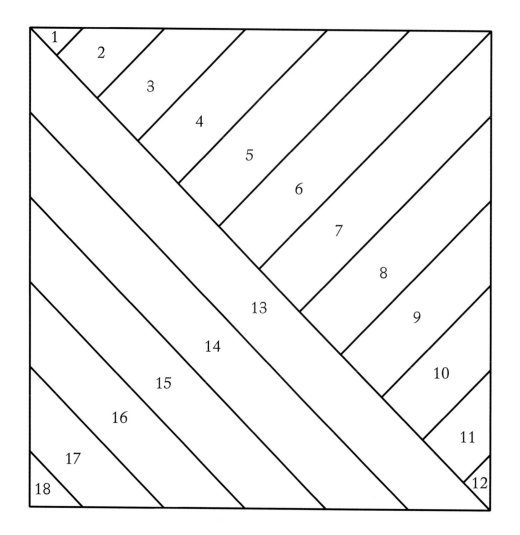

Woven Strips, TRAILING THE SNAIL by Linda Erickson

Border detail for TRAILING THE SNAIL, by Linda J. Erickson. Full quilt shown on page 37.

DESIGN DETAILS

The braids in the border on TRAILING THE SNAIL move around the center with dark and light values meeting along gently curved lines (see quilt photo, page 37). The braided strips are sewn on marked lines for precision, but they can be pieced by using any of the techniques described in Chapter Two, pages 18–21. The corners are designed to frame the quilt asymmetrically.

To fit the border to your quilt, adjust it to the length and width desired.

CONSTRUCTION

1. Prepare foundations for the sides and corners of the quilt.

2. Linda drew the piecing lines for her meandering braid, winding the curved crossing points by alternately angling the braided strips so they were not parallel. To have more structure for the design, draw a horizontal curved line across the approximate center of each foundation.

3. Cut fabric strips with ample seam allowances and piece them by using either top precise pressed-piecing or under pressed-piecing. Begin each border with a triangle to start the braid.

TRAILING THE SNAIL, by Linda J. Erickson, (corner detail). Full quilt on page 37.

Woven Strips, TRAILING THE SNAIL

TRAILING THE SNAIL
partial border pattern

Draw a free-form meander guide line on your foundation to help you place your fabric strips.

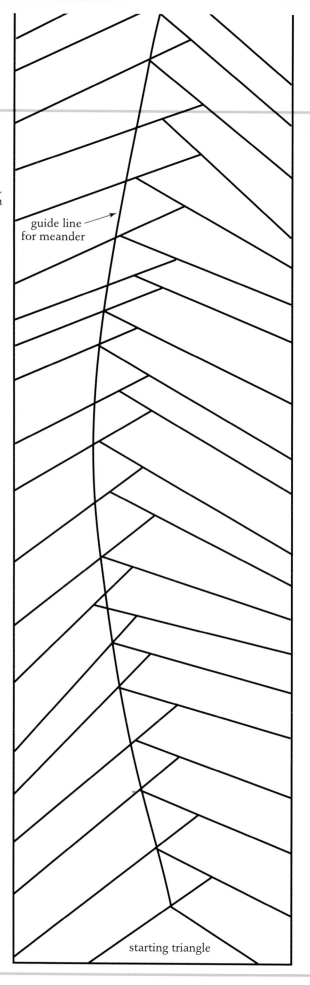

guide line
for meander

FIGURE 4–18. TRAILING THE SNAIL border design. Refer to photo of the full quilt on page 37 to see that Linda colored the braid in each of the border corners differently, forming an asymmetrical light inner border.

starting triangle

Intertwined Strips, WHIRLIGIG by Dixie Haywood

Border detail for WHIRLIGIG, by Dixie Haywood. Full quilt shown on page 43. PHOTO: MELLISA KARLIN MAHONEY

DESIGN DETAILS

The border unit consists of four vertical rows of five squares. There is an additional row at one end of each border to balance the design (Figure 4–19). The arrows in the figure indicate the units. The color sequence alternates in the units, so the border must have an even number of units. The squares in the original border are 1" finished size.

To fit the border to your quilt, do one or both of the following:

1. Enlarge or reduce the squares, which will change the width as well as the length of the border.
2. Add or subtract units in groups of two.

CONSTRUCTION

This border is easiest to construct in long rows. Follow the general checkerboard directions on page 37, with the following changes:

1. The colors are pre-determined and must be carefully marked on the foundation. Double-check to be sure they are in the right position. As a short-cut, mark the interweaving colors in the appropriate squares, leaving the background squares unmarked.
2. If desired, a corner can be pieced on one end of all four borders, rather than on both ends of two borders.
3. Because the borders are identical, you can piece the same row in each border at the same time rather than construct each border individually.

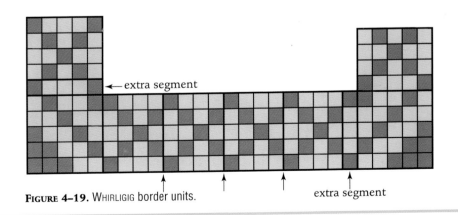

← extra segment

extra segment

FIGURE 4–19. WHIRLIGIG border units.

Strip Patterns
Bargello Borders by Dixie Haywood

Border detail for THE HOWARD FAMILY QUILT, by Dixie Haywood. From the collection of Lance and Dana Howard. Full quilt shown on page 43.

Border detail for SPACE LIGHTS, by Dixie Haywood. Full quilt shown on page 43. PHOTO: MELLISA KARLIN MAHONEY

THE HOWARD FAMILY QUILT, 108" x 108", by Dixie Haywood, (corner detail). Full quilt shown on page 43.

SPACE LIGHTS, 84" x 102", by Dixie Haywood. (corner detail). Full quilt shown on page 43. PHOTO: MELLISA KARLIN MAHONEY

DESIGN DETAILS

The 8"-wide, three-color THE HOWARD FAMILY QUILT border consists of units assembled from four ¾" segments, cut from three different strip-sets (Figure 4–20). The 6"-wide, two-color SPACE LIGHTS border is made of units sewn from six 1" segments, cut from four different strip-sets (Figure 4–21). Arrows in the figures indicate the units. For both quilts, segments are adjusted at the end of each border to balance the design. The corner for each is a Log Cabin block, illustrated on page 43.

To fit either border to a quilt, do one or more of the following:

1. Enlarge or reduce the width of the segments.

2. Add or subtract units.

3. Add or subtract segments at the ends or in the center of the border. See text (page 43) for details on how this was done for SPACE LIGHTS. If you change the cut at the ends of the border, you will have to change the color placement on the corner blocks so the flow around the corner is not disrupted.

CONSTRUCTION

There are several different ways to approach the construction of a strip-set design sewn on foundations. Study the three options on pages 33–36 and decide which one you will use. These directions are basically for the third option and can be adjusted for the other methods.

1. Determine how many segments can be made from each strip-set and the total you will need for all four borders. Prepare a foundation for each strip-set that is as wide as the finished width of the border and as long the fabric strips you will be using (usually cut selvage to selvage).

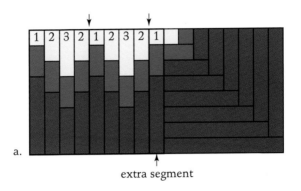

a.

extra segment

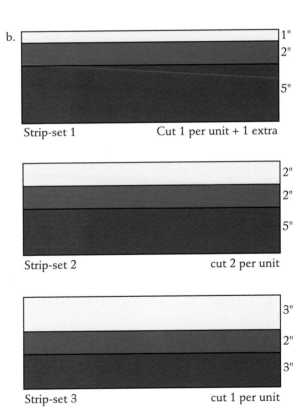

b.

Strip-set 1   Cut 1 per unit + 1 extra

Strip-set 2   cut 2 per unit

Strip-set 3   cut 1 per unit

FIGURE 4–20. (a) THE HOWARD FAMILY QUILT border, (b) three strip-sets.

Bargello Borders

2. Mark the sewing lines on the foundations. If you are making multiples of any strip-set, you can needlepunch the layers. To avoid confusion, write the strip-set number and colors on each foundation. Use under pressed-piecing to sew the strip-set.

3. Cut the strip-set into segments of the desired width. Whether you are drawing cut lines or just using a ruler to cut without marking, take care to cut the segments at a right angle to the seams. It is all too easy to slant the cuts. Carefully remove the freezer paper from the segments and stack them by strip-set in the order they will be sewn.

4. Cut and mark foundations for four corners and four long borders. Take care to keep the lines vertical. To avoid getting a cut out of sequence, mark the cut numbers on the foundation at least at the start of each unit. Stitch the segments on the foundations by using under pressed-piecing, then piece the corner blocks.

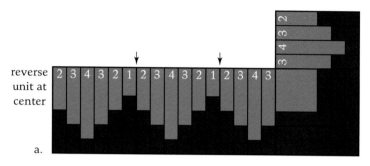

a.

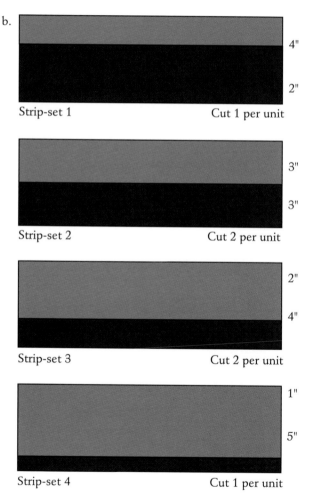

b.

Strip-set 1   Cut 1 per unit

Strip-set 2   Cut 2 per unit

Strip-set 3   Cut 2 per unit

Strip-set 4   Cut 1 per unit

FIGURE 4–21. (a) SPACE LIGHTS border, (b) four strip-sets.

CHAPTER 5

Triangles, Triangles, Triangles

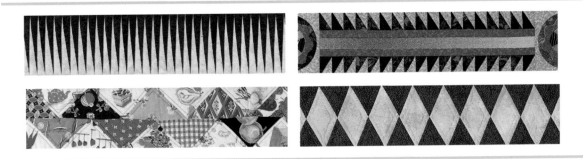

Triangles in one form or another offer myriad choices for border designs. Triangles are more familiar in quilt-speak as Dogtooth, Sawtooth, and Flying Geese, and they are so widely used in one form or another that triangle borders may outnumber those made with other shapes. Their popularity isn't difficult to understand. They are easy to sew, offer interesting variations, and often reinforce shapes and lines from within the quilt top.

An excellent border can be made by repeating a specific triangle from within the quilt. Triangles can be equally effective used singly or in groups, even in a border without the same triangle shape in the body of the quilt. The diagonal lines of a triangle make a pleasing design that will often relate to lines in other parts of the quilt.

The first consideration in making a triangle border is choosing the size and shape of the triangle you will use. Triangles can be compact or elongated, and oriented in different positions to create different effects. They can also be used in combinations and in multiple rows.

The three basic types of triangles are equilateral,

isosceles, and asymmetrical. An equilateral triangle, usually seen in Dogtooth borders, has three identical sides and angles. The most commonly used border triangle, however, is the isosceles triangle, which has two identical sides and angles. The half-square, right-angled triangle is an example of an isosceles triangle. It has two equal sides with two 45° angles and one 90° right angle (Figure 5–1). It can be used for Dogtooth, Sawtooth, and Flying Geese borders. Triangles are not always so simply defined, however. The angles and lengths of sides can vary in infinite combinations, creating asymmetric as well as

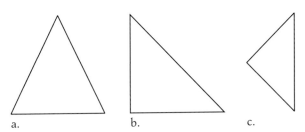

FIGURE 5–1. Triangle types: (a) Dogtooth, (b) Sawtooth, (c) Flying Geese.

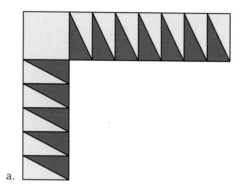

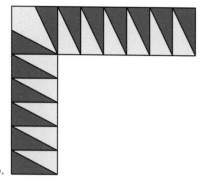

FIGURE 5–2. Triangle orientation: (a) pointing outward, (b) pointing inward.

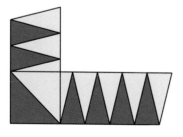

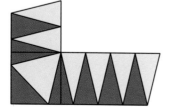

FIGURE 5–3. Possible corner alignments.

classic shapes. Your choices are limited only by your imagination.

Another major design decision for a triangle border is its orientation. Do you want the base or the point of the major-colored triangle to be aligned with the edge of the quilt top? Will the major color be at the outside or the inside edge of the border (Figure 5–2)? The setting will affect the focus of your border and may affect the corner design. The effect is strikingly different in each case. Any of the triangular border patterns at the end of this chapter can be set facing either inward or outward.

DOGTOOTH TRIANGLES

Dogtooth borders made from isosceles triangles are the simplest to fit along a border because their measurements are easily varied; that is, the base of the triangle can be contracted or expanded to fit into the border length. You can determine the triangle's base measurement by simple division or by folding and refolding a piece of paper, cut the length of the border, into smaller sections. The width of the border can be adjusted by extending the height of the triangles. Within these parameters, there usually are many possible unit sizes. You should choose the best proportion of triangle height to base for your quilt.

When using a Dogtooth border, you need to consider how the design will turn the corners. Decide whether the base or the point of the triangle will align with the corner of the quilt top. This decision will impact the design of the corner but will not affect the rest of the border design (Figure 5–3).

The simple Dogtooth border was often used successfully to frame nineteenth-century appliqué designs. These borders were usually appliquéd on the background fabric, with the bases of the isosceles triangles at the edge of the quilt. We find it easier and more efficient to piece them by machine on marked foundations.

The Dogtooth border in Dixie's ANNIVERSARY STAR echoes the many points within the quilt,

Photo 5–1. Border detail for Anniversary Star, 47" x 47", by Dixie Haywood.

which are softened by the curves of the pattern (Photo 5–1). The major color points into the quilt, expanding the light background beyond the square of the quilt body, while the final darker single-fabric border provides a solid base for the slender Dogtooth triangles. The points of the colored triangles align with the edge of the quilt top, so the corner, in effect, contains the other half of the triangle.

Dixie designed the border for Jinnianna to repeat the woven effect of the medallion in the body of the quilt (Photo 5–2, page 60). It illustrates several adjustments that may be necessary in planning a border. To turn the corner smoothly, the design has to change direction in the center of the border. A narrow red border, called a "spacer," had to be added to the edge of the quilt top to create a common unit measurement, but the color choice makes it seem a natural transition to the border.

Los Ventos is a two-color quilt that began as an experiment in piecing a Mariner's Compass design on foundations (Photo 5–3, page 60). Jane originally began with a limited amount of fabric from her stash, not dreaming that she would end up with a full-sized quilt. She used all of the fabric for the nine large blocks. The piece was too big for a wallhanging and too small for a bed quilt, so she used a point from the compass block to design the border. The points are directed toward the outside of the quilt.

Anniversary Star, 47" x 47", by Dixie Haywood.

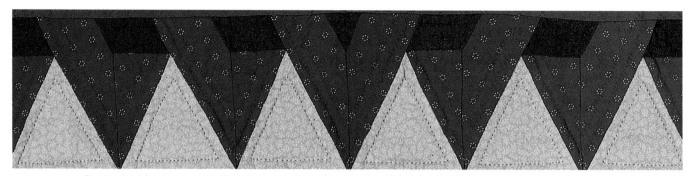

PHOTO 5–2. Border detail for JINNIANNA, by Dixie Haywood. From the collection of Judith A. McNickle.

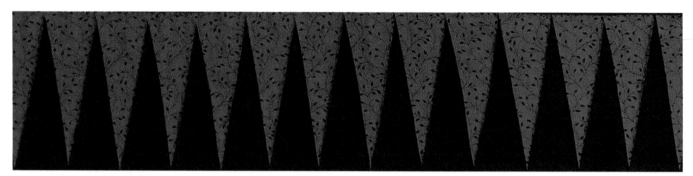

PHOTO 5–3. Border detail for LOS VENTOS, by Jane Hall.

JINNIANNA, 40" x 46", by Dixie Haywood.
From the collection of Judith A. McNickle.

LOS VENTOS, 73" x 84", by Jane Hall.

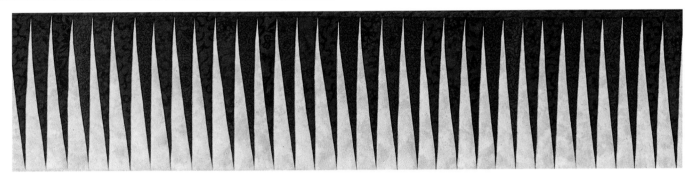

Photo 5–4. Border detail for Indigo, by Jane Hall.

This border made the quilt larger, but it was still square and still too small for a bed. Jane added double black-and-red strips of varying widths to each side, and triple strips to the top and bottom edges. These additions lengthened the quilt and provided a strong frame with the long vertical lines of color. Small Mariner's Compass blocks, replicating the larger ones from inside the quilt, completed the corners.

Along the way, she ran out of not only the red, but also the black fabric, so there are many different fabric dye lots in the quilt. The differences are not readily apparent because the fabrics are separated from each other by borders of the opposite color. The combination of border designs makes the quilt more interesting than perhaps it would have been if she hadn't run out of fabric.

Jane's Indigo is another two-color quilt, although there are several different indigo fabrics in the compass blocks. The design has long skinny points, which she wanted to repeat in the border. Using one point from the compass, with a 7⁄8" base and a 6" height, she first tried the border design with the dark triangles against the body of the quilt. Ultimately, she reversed the design so that the dark points come into the quilt border from the outer edge (Photo 5–4).

The corners presented a particular challenge. Jane found that the best way to deal with designing them was to draw different possibilities on

Indigo, 72" x 90", by Jane Hall.

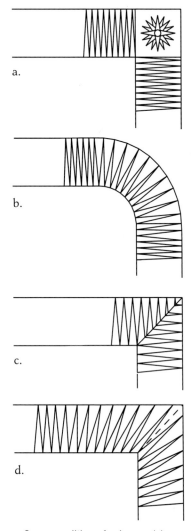

a.

b.

c.

d.

FIGURE 5–4. Corner auditions for INDIGO: (a) separate corner design, (b) rounded corners with radiating points, (c) mitered corner, (d) points swaying into corner.

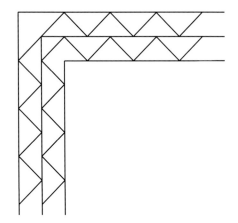

FIGURE 5–5. Zigzag border design.

strips of paper that were cut as full-sized corners. She tried several designs in different arrangements (Figure 5–4). She settled on having the points "sway" into the corners, beginning their slant a few inches before the corner on each side. Mathematics helped, but, in the end, actually seeing the way the points went around the corners was the deciding factor.

Susan Dague used right-angled triangles in a variation of the Dogtooth design in FOOD QUILT: IN MY GRANDMOTHER'S KITCHEN (Photo 5–5). Large triangles, laid on their long sides, are the same size as one element of the square-in-square blocks. By dovetailing light and dark triangles in two offset rows, she created a streak-of-lightning pattern that mirrored the light, vertical streaks of lightning running through the quilt top (Figure 5–5).

The design zigzags around the quilt, turning the corners smoothly, and is contained by a small inner border of red-checked fabric. The inner border was a late design decision. Susan says, "After the border was constructed and sewn to the quilt, the edge of the quilt was a muddle of triangles. Neither the border nor the blocks were easily discernible. Adding the bright inner border necessitated re-drafting the corner squares to a new, larger size. The real plus was how easy this fix was, because I was using foundations."

SAMARKAND, by Virginia Siciliano, has a large-scale Dogtooth border, feathered with the same small half-square triangles that edge the stars in her Pine Burr blocks (Photo 5–6). Virginia says, "Truly effective borders enhance and complement the body of the quilt. They should not be an afterthought but should be an integral extension of the design." She wanted the stars to float in the center of the quilt and decided they needed a substantial border to balance their weight and complexity. She believes, "One must think of a quilt design as a musical composition and give it a beautiful ending."

Inspired by a graphic wallhanging with arcs and circles, Kathy Butts made KATHERINE CONNER'S WHEELS in honor of her maternal grandmother

Photo 5–5. Border detail for Food Quilt: In My Grandmother's Kitchen, by Susan Dague.

Photo 5–6. Border detail for Samarkand, by Virginia Siciliano, pattern by Karen Stone.

Food Quilt: In My Grandmother's Kitchen, 73" x 84",
by Susan Dague.

Samarkand, 82" x 82", by Virginia Siciliano, pattern by Karen Stone.

(Photo 5–7). The circles represent the wheels the grandmother used in her lifetime, including her trek in a covered wagon from Pennsylvania to Nebraska. The spikes and peaks of the border reflect her journey to Colorado after her marriage, with the final blue border representing the sky over Colorado. As a young girl, Katherine remembers her grandmother telling her, "The sky's the limit." She says, "My grandmother was a quilter, and I hope she approves of my telling her life in a quilt."

The work of Caryl Bryer Fallert inspired Kathy's dynamic curved pieced border. She goes on to say, "I knew that these spikes and peaks would have to be foundation pieced, this being the easiest and most accurate way of doing them because each piece was a different shape and size. (I hate working with a lot of templates.) I first drew the curve on one quarter of a side of the quilt and divided it into sections for piecing. I copied the

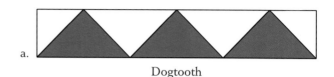

a.

Dogtooth

b.

Sawtooth

c.

Asymmetrical Sawtooth

FIGURE 5–6. Right-angle triangles: (a) Dogtooth, (b) Sawtooth, (c) Asymmetrical Sawtooth.

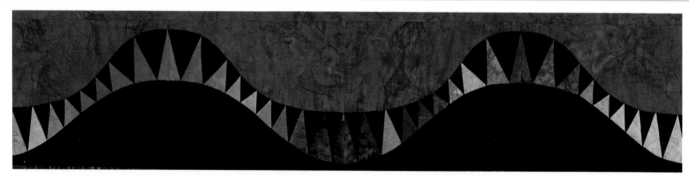

PHOTO 5–7. Border detail for KATHERINE CONNOR'S WHEELS, by Kathy Butts. Quilt pattern by Wendy Hager. Full quilt shown on page 65.
PHOTO: MELLISA KARLIN MAHONEY

PHOTO 5–8. Border detail for MADAME PRESIDENT, by Dixie Haywood and friends. Full quilt shown on page 65.

sections so I had all four quarters. I did have to fudge a bit and stretch or shrink a section or two to make the border fit the quilt. The hardest part was sequencing the colors to fit the border."

SAWTOOTH TRIANGLES

Right-angle, half-square triangles can be used in a Dogtooth configuration, as shown in the previous quilts (Figure 5–6a). They are more commonly used in Sawtooth borders, a perennial favorite because of its adaptability and ease of construction (Figure 5–6b). The corners for Sawtooth borders are not complicated and can often be pieced as part of the border foundation.

A Sawtooth design lends itself to a variety of combinations, multiplications, and alignments, both simple and intricate. Sometimes the triangles are large and form the only border, sometimes they are small and used as an inner border. Usually the right-angle triangle has equal legs, but to make a wider border, the triangle can be stretched into an elongated shape (Figure 5–6c). The measurement for both base and height will depend on the size of the desired border, as well as the effect you are seeking.

MADAME PRESIDENT is a quilt Dixie made from the blocks her guild members traditionally make for their outgoing president. A Sawtooth border was a natural for these blocks (Photo 5–8). This busy scrap quilt needed a finish, not an additional statement. The border units are half the size of the blocks, a satisfactory proportion and a comfort to work with after the intricacies of designing the layout of the quilt and the lettering.

The major-color triangles in MADAME PRESIDENT point inward, seeming to contain the design. In contrast, the tiny triangles in Lynne Harrill's Sawtooth border on her RED FEATHERS quilt point outward, expanding this miniature quilt's importance (Photo 5–9, page 66). The effect is amplified by reversing the direction of the triangles in the center of each border and by repeating the size and colors of the triangles used for the feathered star. The

KATHERINE CONNOR'S WHEELS, 86" x 94", by Kathy Butts. Quilt pattern by Wendy Hager. PHOTO: MELLISA KARLIN MAHONEY

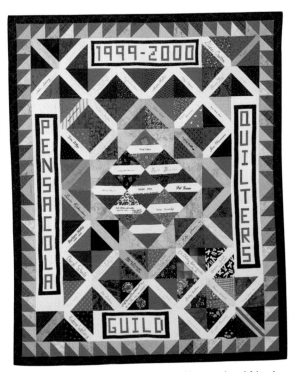

MADAME PRESIDENT, 66" x 80", by Dixie Haywood and friends.

PHOTO 5–9. Border detail for RED FEATHERS, by Lynne G. Harrill. Full quilt shown on page 67.

PHOTO 5–10. Border detail for CALYPSO, by Susan C. Derkacz. Full quilt shown on page 67.

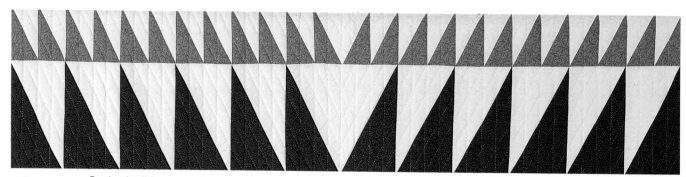

PHOTO 5–11. Border detail for JOHN'S MICHIGAN MEMORIES, by Debra Ballard. Full quilt shown on page 67.

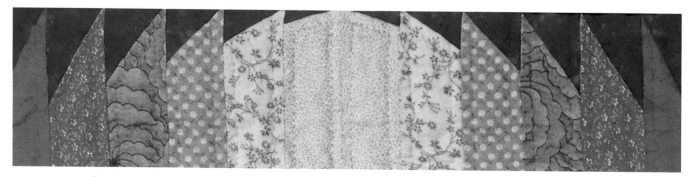

PHOTO 5–12. Border detail for SAGAN'S SUNRISE, by Bette Haddon. Full quilt shown on page 68.

inner and outer borders of background fabric float the Sawtooth border and the star, making a fine example of "less is more."

Susan Derkacz's CALYPSO has double rows of Sawtooth triangles for both sashing and borders, creating an exciting contrast to the curves of the appliqué design (Photo 5–10). Repeating the centers of the block motif in the cornerstones gives them a major design importance. The mirror-image Sawtooth borders separated by strips of color from the quilt add strength and balance to this contemporary reincarnation of the classic four-block quilt and are in keeping with the tradition of pieced sashing and borders for appliqué quilts. Susan remarks, "The foundation piecing made the compound sashing very accurate and easy to put the quilt together."

Debra Ballard used long-legged sawteeth in two sizes to frame her medallion quilt, JOHN'S MICHIGAN MEMORIES (Photo 5–11). The center and corner designs were inspired by an antique quilt, and she hand-appliquéd motifs from her son's childhood in the background areas. The large triangles in the border are twice the size of the small outer ones, which slows down the movement and makes a strong graphic frame. The color changes between the Sawtooth borders echo those within the quilt, with the lighter ones in the last border containing the larger dark border. Susan turned the border corners skillfully, showcasing comparable motifs from the center of the quilt.

Bette Haddon uses another Sawtooth variation in her quilt SAGAN'S SUNRISE, dedicated to the memory of Carl Sagan (Photo 5–12). The elongated Sawtooth angles of each triangle are incrementally changed to morph into bargello-like units, grading the colors from the quilt dark to light to dark again, which creates depth and dimension. The units at the end of each border are mitered to create an effective corner design. Bette chose to use half units at the top of the side borders to maintain a constant unit size, rather than to adjust the width of the individual patches to complete the design motif at each corner.

RED FEATHERS, 11" x 19", by Lynne G. Harrill.

CALYPSO, 83" x 83", by Susan C. Derkacz.

JOHN'S MICHIGAN MEMORIES, 90" x 90", by Debra Ballard.

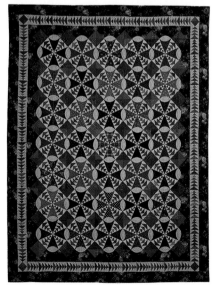

SAGAN'S SUNRISE, 80" x 90", by Bette Haddon. Detail on page 66.

GEESE TRAILS, 24" x 24", by Jane Hall. PHOTO: MELLISA KARLIN MAHONEY

OAK AND SUMAC, 84" x 110", by Dixie Haywood.
PHOTO: MELLISA KARLIN MAHONEY

FLYING GEESE TRIANGLES

Dogtooth and Sawtooth borders are fairly descriptive of their profile, but there is instant recognition of the reason the Flying Geese pattern is so named. Right-angle triangles are turned so the long sides are vertical, giving the appearance of a flock of geese flying in a "V" formation. There is a sense of movement regardless of how the design is arranged. It can travel in one direction around the entire quilt or change direction in the center of each border, flying either toward the center or toward the corners (Figure 5–7).

There are three right-angle triangles in one unit of this pattern, with a small background triangle on either side of a large central one. The standard unit is twice as high as it is wide, so an adjustment in one measurement needs to be doubled or halved in the other. Like the other triangle configurations, multiple rows of the same size or proportional enlargements of the design offer useful and attractive possibilities. Tweaking one or more of the angles makes it possible to change the unit dimension and the resulting graphic effect.

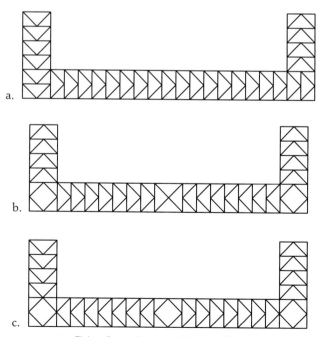

FIGURE 5–7. Flying Geese borders: (a) encircling the quilt, (b) flying toward the middle of the border, (c) flying toward the corner.

PHOTO 5–13. Border detail for GEESE TRAILS, by Jane Hall. Full quilt shown on page 68. PHOTO: MELLISA KARLIN MAHONEY

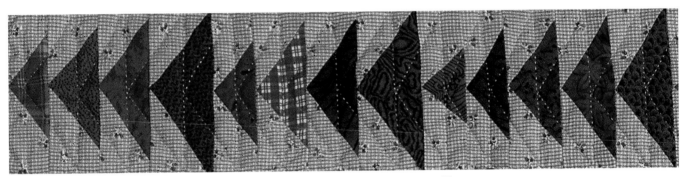

PHOTO 5–14. Border detail for OAK AND SUMAC, by Dixie Haywood. Full quilt shown on page 68. PHOTO: MELLISA KARLIN MAHONEY

In Jane's GEESE TRAILS, she wanted a small border of Flying Geese set within a wide border of the print from the quilt blocks (Photo 5–13). The Flying Geese enclose the quilt in a lattice design, rather than making a square frame with separate corners. This involved using dimensions for the plain borders that were multiples of the Flying Geese units, both in height and in width, to work out the fit. Because the Flying Geese unit was so small, she used a thin tracing paper for the foundation so it would tear out easily.

The graduated Flying Geese in the OAK AND SUMAC blocks inspired Dixie to use the same arrangement for the middle border. The border geese flow in one direction around the quilt with the square-on-point blocks repeated in the corners (Photo 5–14). Because the angles of the Flying Geese triangles change, the width of the border was not limited by the two-to-one ratio of the traditional unit measurements. The five Flying Geese in the blocks are repeated in the border, with segments of varying widths forming a border unit 6" long by 4" wide. By adjusting the width of the first border, on which extensions of the block were appliquéd to complete the graphics of the pattern, Dixie was able to devise a common unit measurement. This design required leaving out the largest segment of the unit at the end of each of the borders.

Jennifer Amor's clever adaptation of the Flying Geese pattern in her TOUCAN TANGO quilt (first in a series of "Happy Quilts") is perfect for her festive tropical theme, and it shows the versatility of this simple triangle turned into "wacky" geese (Photo 5–15, page 70). The curving bands of triangles are appliquéd on the wide blue border, balancing the center appliqué. Accenting the geese with a narrow strip of bright, contrasting fabric provides additional color and movement that fairly dances around the border. You can almost hear a steel band playing.

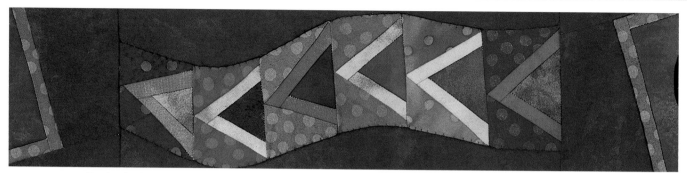

PHOTO 5–15. Border detail for TOUCAN TANGO, by Jennifer Amor.

PHOTO 5–16. Border detail for UZBEK ARROWHEADS, by Jane Hall.

TOUCAN TANGO, 22" x 24", by Jennifer Amor.

UZBEK ARROWHEADS, 24" x 24", by Jane Hall.

PHOTO 5–17. Border detail for GOLDEN TWILIGHT, by Marlene Royse.

Jane's UZBEK ARROWHEADS border on the small Mariner's Compass is a form of Flying Geese in which the triangles are almost equilateral instead of the usual two-to-one format (Photo 5–16). Designs like these, common in central Asia, can be used as borders and accents on quilts and wearables. Jane pieced the design on long strips of tracing paper. Because of the small size of the triangles, she allowed an extra 1/8" on each side of the pieced strip, making the geese appear to float in the border.

After making a 50th anniversary quilt for her parents, Marlene Royse had an ample supply of gold fabrics on hand, so she used them with purple and black stars for GOLDEN TWILIGHT (Photo 5–17). The border design, combining two of the three major triangle border arrangements, came from a workshop she took with Cindy Blackberg. Marlene pieced the Flying Geese strip with a dark triangle on the side closest to the body of the quilt and a light triangle on the opposite side. This arrangement creates a strong Sawtooth frame, which is interwoven with the large, pale Flying Geese triangles. The overall effect is that of motion and counterpoint as the Sawtooth triangles rotate against the Flying Geese.

BEYOND BASIC TRIANGLES

To this point, we have been describing triangles in three traditional configurations for border designs, but the versatility of this shape goes far

beyond these basic patterns. Like children's puzzle blocks, triangles can be combined with themselves or with other geometric shapes to create new designs that relate well to the basic triangle. Colorations can produce an interwoven effect and add the illusion of depth and dimension.

The border for PARADISE contains only triangles, but it includes Sawtooth, Dogtooth, and Flying Geese configurations (Photo 5–18, page 72).

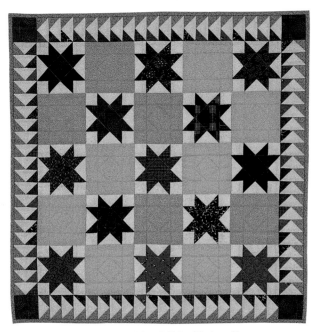

GOLDEN TWILIGHT, 24" x 24", by Marlene Royse.

PHOTO 5–18. Border detail for PARADISE, by Jane Hall. Full quilt shown on page 73.

PHOTO 5–19. Border detail for CHROMANIA TOO, by Dixie Haywood. Full quilt shown on page 73.

PHOTO 5–20. Border detail for A TAD PLAID, by Dixie Haywood. From the collection of Cedar Howard. Full quilt shown on page 73.
PHOTO: MELLISA KARLIN MAHONEY

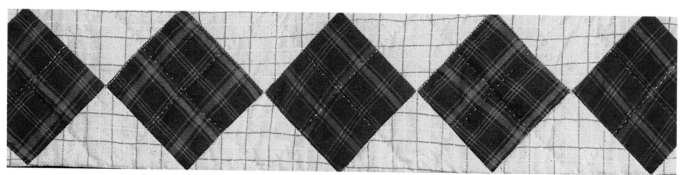

PHOTO 5–21. Border detail for HOT COTTON, by Dixie Haywood. Full quilt shown on page 74.

The Flying Geese-like triangles are made from bits of hand-dyed fabrics left over from piecing the quilt. Jane placed them around the border to match the interior color changes. They create an illusion of depth and make the pattern appear to change as the color changes. The corners all but designed themselves, with small half-square triangles used in the appropriate colors to turn onto the next side smoothly.

CHROMANIA TOO and PARADISE have a piecing sequence in common and a similar look, both appearing more complex than they, in fact, are. Instead of using only triangles, Dixie created the border of CHROMANIA TOO from triangles and angled strips (Photo 5–19). Using all the colors in the crazy-pieced curved nine-patch in the center adds a unity needed by this small quilt.

Squares on-point and diamonds both relate to triangles, not only because they can be divided in half or quarters to form triangles, but also because their diagonal lines create some of the same graphic impact that triangles give to a design. Dividing them into triangles can enrich the shapes by allowing more fabrics to be used to form the larger shape. In addition, triangles are usually needed to complete any designs that contain both squares on-point and diamonds, cementing the connection between them.

The border in Dixie's A TAD PLAID has no obvious connection to the shapes within the quilt, although turning squares on-point is a subtle and pleasing design link (Photo 5–20). Using the same plaids throughout the border provides cohesion to this scrap quilt of plaid and striped fabrics. The red plaid is used in the small cornerstones of the sashing and in some of the blocks. The light plaid, also used in the blocks, frames and brightens the quilt while maintaining its appeal for the teenage grandson for whom it was made.

To piece the border, the foundation had to be cut into segments, after marking. This is an example of a design in which the unit measurement for fit-

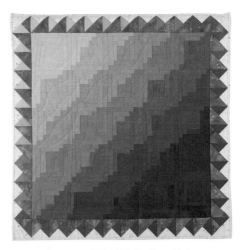

PARADISE, 30" x 30", by Jane Hall.

CHROMANIA TOO, 16" x 16", by Dixie Haywood.

A TAD PLAID, 68" x 85", by Dixie Haywood.
From the collection of Cedar Howard. PHOTO: MELLISA KARLIN MAHONEY

HOT COTTON, 94" x 94", by Dixie Haywood.

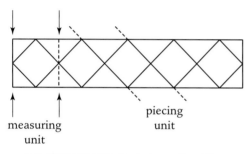

measuring
unit

piecing
unit

FIGURE 5–8. Notice that the measuring unit and the piecing unit differ.

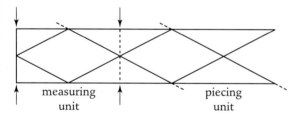

measuring
unit

piecing
unit

FIGURE 5–9. Another example of different measuring and piecing units.

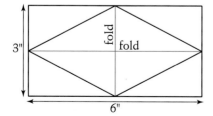

3"

fold

fold

6"

FIGURE 5–10. Drawing a diamond to any size: cut a piece of paper the size of the unit, fold it in half in both directions, draw lines connecting the ends of the folds.

ting the border is not the same as the measurement for the pieced unit. The border units are 3½" squares, which consist of the square on-point surrounded by triangles. The piecing unit, however, is a rhomboid that includes a square and two triangles (Figure 5–8). Be aware that many border designs, especially those including triangles, require this mental shift between figuring the border dimensions and piecing it.

HOT COTTON is another example of differing measuring units and piecing units (Figure 5–9, Photo 5–21, detail page 72). Also, like A TAD PLAID, the fabric rather than the shape provides a connection to the quilt design. The impact of this traditional Cotton Boll pattern is so strong that Dixie wanted a similarly strong angled shape to contrast with the curves. Using the same diamond dimensions in the sashing and the border avoided fragmenting the design of the two elements, while changing the orientation of these diamonds achieved a proportional difference between the two.

Diamonds, like triangles, can have angle adjustments. The angles do not have to be the usual 45°, 60°, and 90°. To fit both the blocks and the border with the same diamond, Dixie found that a common measurement was more important than a common angle. The 24" blocks have four 3" x 6" units arranged horizontally. When the units were turned vertically to form a 6"-wide border, they still fit the 24" blocks as well as the 3" sashing. The diamond and triangle dimensions were determined by folding a 3" x 6" paper in quarters and connecting the ends of the fold lines with drawn lines (Figure 5–10). The angles are irrelevant; the fit is not.

Simple Dogtooth, ANNIVERSARY STAR by Dixie Haywood

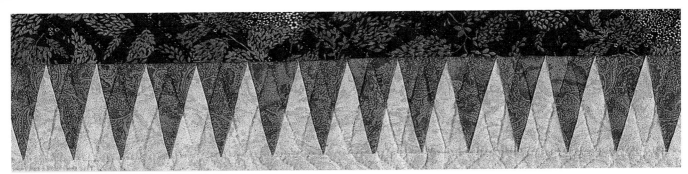

Border detail for ANNIVERSARY STAR, by Dixie Haywood. Full quilt shown on page 59.

DESIGN DETAILS

This 3"-wide border contains isosceles triangles with a 1¼" base. The triangles extend into two sides of the corners, with a right-angle triangle connecting their bases (Figure 5–11).

To fit the border to your quilt, do one or both of the following:

1. Enlarge or reduce the base of the triangles.

2. Lengthen or shorten the sides of the triangles.

CONSTRUCTION

1. Prepare four border foundations from the pattern on page 76. Include one corner section in each foundation.

2. Use rough-cut templates (page 22) to cut fabric pieces. Piece each border by using under pressed-piecing.

3. To sew the borders to the quilt, start and end each seam at the corner triangles, but do not sew into the seam allowances. Sew the angled seams between the borders without stitching across the allowances where the seams meet.

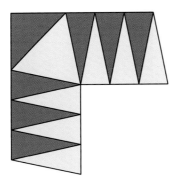

FIGURE 5–11. ANNIVERSARY STAR border design (pattern on page 76).

3"-WIDE BORDER

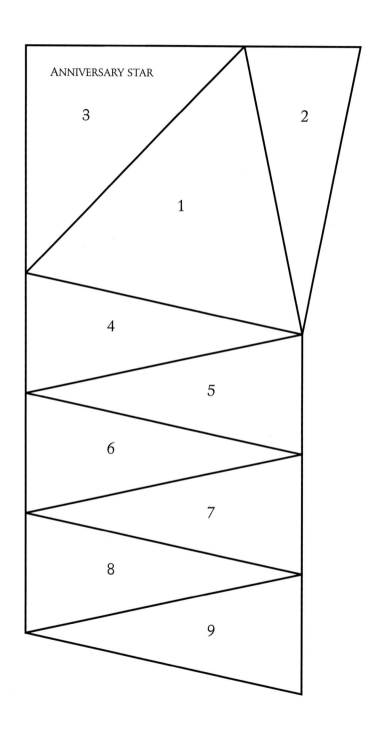

ANNIVERSARY STAR

3

2

1

4

5

6

7

8

9

Woven Dogtooth, JINNIANNA by Dixie Haywood

Border detail for JINNIANNA, by Dixie Haywood. From the collection of Judith A. McNickle. Full quilt shown on page 60.

DESIGN DETAILS

This 5"-wide border is made of asymmetrical 4" units and 5" corners. The units are reversed in the center of each border (Figure 5–12).

To fit the border to your quilt, do one or both of the following:

1. Extend the legs of the triangles for a wider border.

2. Compress or expand the units.

CONSTRUCTION

1. Prepare four corner unit and center unit foundations, along with the number of border unit foundations needed. Half of the border unit foundations must be reversed. If you are needle-punching freezer paper, layer half of the foundations shiny side up and the other half shiny side down. Accordion-pleating a long strip of freezer paper will accomplish the same thing.

2. Cut the fabric pieces with rough-cut templates (page 22), but remember that half of the asymmetrical pieces must be reversed. Sew on the foundations by using under pressed-piecing.

3. Trim the excess fabric extending beyond the foundations to a ¼" seam allowance and join the units to form four borders by sewing corners to each end of two borders. Attach the side borders to the quilt first, then the top and bottom borders.

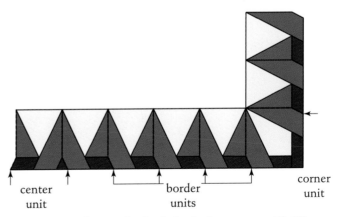

center unit — border units — corner unit

FIGURE 5–12. JINNIANNA border design (pattern on pages 78–80).

5"-WIDE BORDER

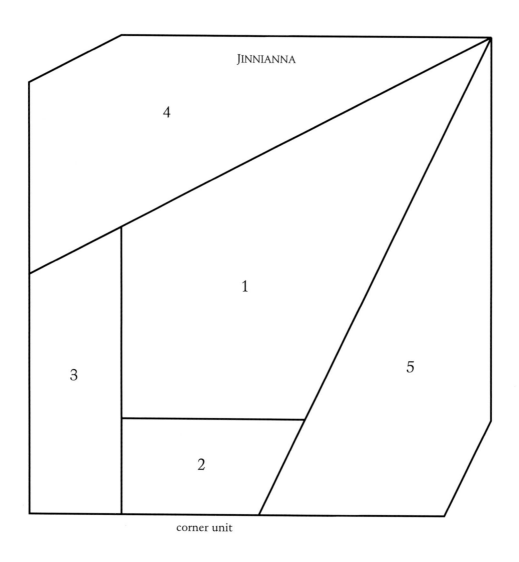

JINNIANNA

4

1

3

5

2

corner unit

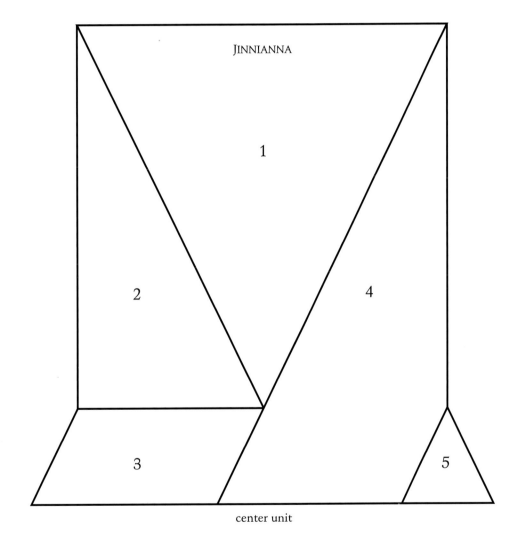

JINNIANNA

center unit

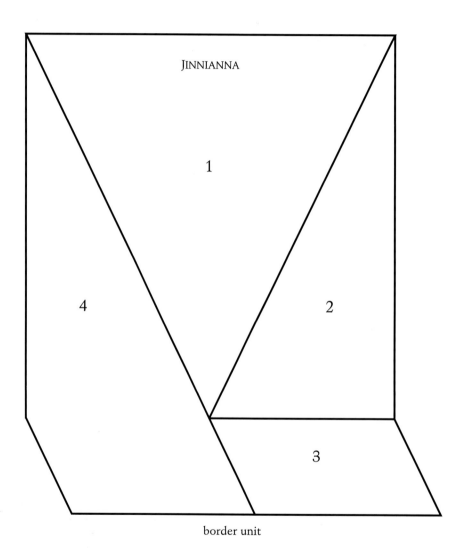

JINNIANNA

1

4

2

3

border unit

Long Narrow Dogtooth, INDIGO by Jane Hall

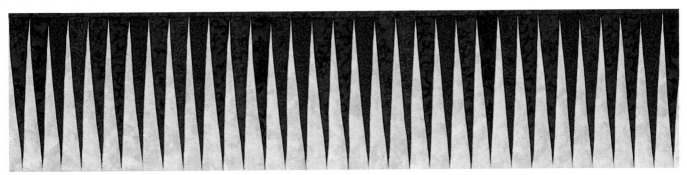

Border detail for INDIGO, by Jane Hall. Full quilt shown on page 61.

DESIGN DETAILS

For this border, long points from the compass block are set side by side, with the bases of the points at the outside edge. The points sway into the corners, beginning their slant about 6" from the inside corners (Figure 5–13).

To fit the border to your quilt, divide the border measurement evenly into small equal sections (for example 1"). The division size is the base measurement for the border triangles. To design the corner, you will need to experiment with different widths for both background points and compass points, slanting them to fit the area.

For INDIGO, Jane started drafting the swaying points 6" away from the inside border corner. She divided the 6" space into 10 increments that became smaller as they approached the corner; that is, the base triangle measurement was decreased from ⅞" to ¾", ⅝", ½", and finally ⅜".

On the outside border edge, she started 1" on each side of the corner and divided the area into increments that were larger nearest to the corner. By connecting these inside and outside edge marks, the compass points became slanted. Jane made

slight adjustments in the drafting until the proportions were pleasing. These general directions are applicable to almost any other triangle shapes used in a border.

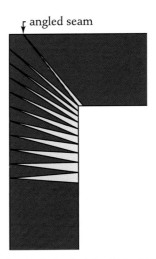

FIGURE 5–13. INDIGO border design (point pattern on page 82).

POINT ⅞" x 6"

INDIGO

CONSTRUCTION

1. Prepare four freezer-paper border foundations. The corners were drawn and sewn so that the angles were included in the border foundations. Notice in the figure on page 81 that the angled seam is slightly off to one side so the center corner triangle will not be split.

2. Draw the compass points on the dull side of the foundations. For ease of fitting the points into the border evenly, begin marking the lines in the middle of the border, adjusting the divisions slightly if needed as you reach the ends.

3. Using rough-cut templates, cut stacks of point shapes from several of the fabrics used in the quilt. Select the fabrics randomly. Use under pressed-piecing, beginning at one end of each border foundation, to sew the foundations.

4. As each border is completed, stitch a 2" piece of solid fabric on the outer edge to contain the stretchy points. This fabric will ultimately become part of the binding, but it will serve to stabilize the points after the borders have been joined to the quilt and the foundations removed.

Flying Geese, GEESE TRAILS by Jane Hall

Border detail for GEESE TRAILS, by Jane Hall. Full quilt shown on page 68. PHOTO: MELLISA KARLIN MAHONEY

DESIGN DETAILS

Flying Geese units are classically drawn with the short side being half the measurement of the long side. This wallhanging has lines of small Flying Geese set into a single-fabric border. The top and bottom rows of geese cross over the side rows, creating a lattice effect at the corners (Figure 5–14). Thin tracing paper was chosen as a foundation because it would tear out easily and would not create extra weight when the pieced border was set into the single-fabric border.

To fit the border to your quilt, use the following suggestions:

○ Measure the quilt top to find a unit size that will divide evenly into the border length and that will produce Flying Geese of the appropriate proportion.

○ Determine where in the wide border you will place the strip of Flying Geese. It may be necessary to use a spacer border to create a measurement that's easy to divide evenly. The finished width of this single-fabric spacer strip must be a multiple of the short side of the Flying Geese unit.

○ If you look at Figure 5–14, you will see that one Flying Geese unit fits at the end of the spacer border. The outer single-fabric strip should be a multiple of that measurement, depending on the number of Flying Geese units you want to put at the ends of the border strip.

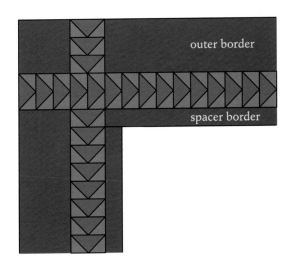

FIGURE 5–14. GEESE TRAILS border design (pattern on page 84).

CONSTRUCTION

1. Referring to Figure 5–15, stitch spacer borders, cut 1¼" wide to finish ¾", to the quilt top.

2. Draw the Flying Geese units, ¾" by 1½", on thin tracing paper foundations. Because the geese fly toward the border centers, each border must be pieced in two segments and joined after piecing. You will also need four small foundations of Flying Geese units for the corners.

3. For the large geese triangles, cut quarter-square triangles from 3¼" squares, and half-square triangles for the background triangles from 2" squares. For the outer borders, cut four 2¾" corner squares and four 2¾"-wide single-fabric strips.

4. Sew the triangles to the foundations by using under pressed-piecing. Join the border halves so the geese are flying toward each other. Assemble the corner pieces.

5. Sew a Flying Geese border to two opposite sides of the quilt. Add a 2¾" single-fabric outer border to these two attached Flying Geese borders.

6. Stitch the top and bottom pieced Flying Geese borders to the quilt, matching the side border seams where the geese cross.

7. Assemble the top and bottom borders as shown in Figure 5–15, then sew them to the quilt. Be sure to match the cross seams carefully.

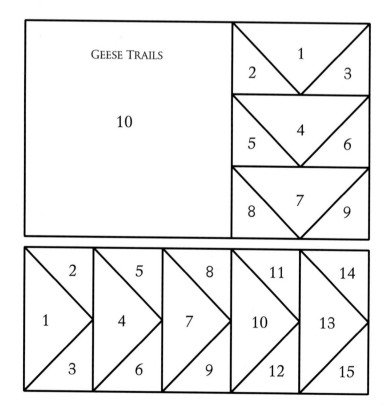

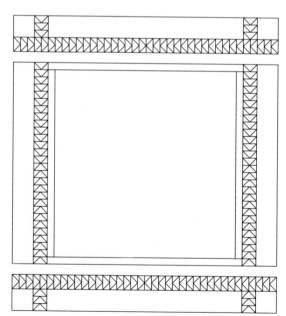

FIGURE 5–15. Quilt Assembly.

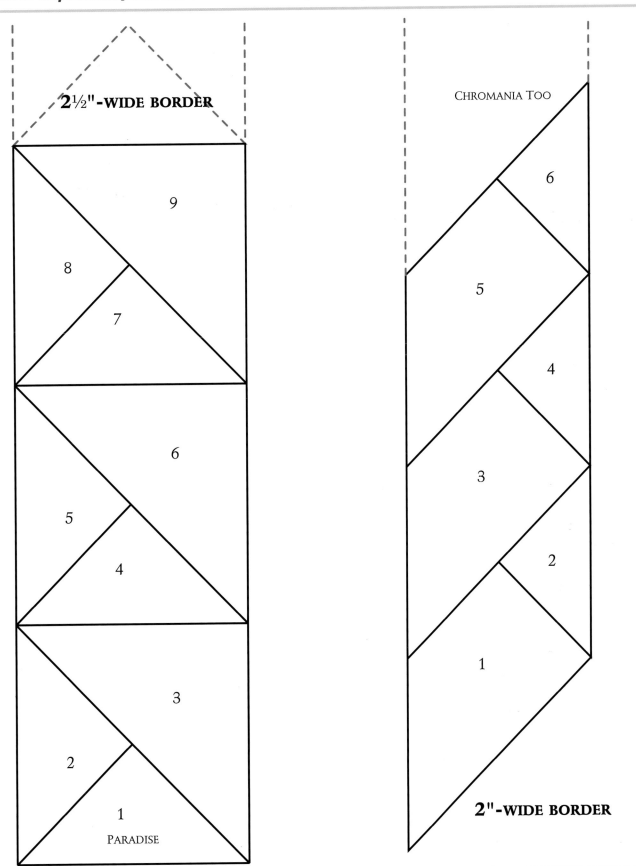

2½"-WIDE BORDER

CHROMANIA TOO

9

8

7

6

5

4

3

2

1

PARADISE

6

5

4

3

2

1

2"-WIDE BORDER

Strips and Triangles, CHROMANIA TOO by Dixie Haywood

Border detail for CHROMANIA TOO, by Dixie Haywood. Full quilt shown on page 73.

DESIGN DETAILS

This mitered border, wraps around the quilt in a continuous braid-like pattern (Figure 5–21).

To fit the border to your quilt, enlarge or reduce the measuring unit square. This will change the width as well as the length of the border.

CONSTRUCTION

1. Prepare four full-length mitered border foundations. The border will be reversed from the tracing pattern, which is not important so long as all four foundations are identical.

2. Cut fabric in strips and use the quick-cutting method to cut the triangles.

3. Use under pressed-piecing to sew the triangles to the foundations.

4. Attach the borders to the quilt and miter the corners.

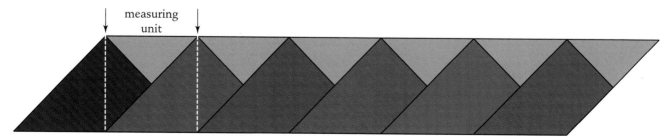

FIGURE 5–21. CHROMANIA TOO border design (pattern on page 89).

Square On-Point, A TAD PLAID by Dixie Haywood

Border detail for A TAD PLAID, by Dixie Haywood. From the collection of Cedar Howard. Full quilt shown on page 73. PHOTO: MELLISA KARLIN MAHONEY

DESIGN DETAILS

The border is based on a 3½" square grid. It is pieced in rhomboid-shaped segments (Figure 5–22).

To fit the border to your quilt, enlarge or reduce the square grid. This will change the width as well as the length of the border.

CONSTRUCTION

1. Prepare border foundations and cut fabric pieces. Two corner units will be included on each end of two of the border foundations.

2. Cut the border into piecing sections and sew with under pressed-piecing. It is fast and easy to chain-stitch the sections before cutting, pressing, and adding the next patch.

3. Trim the fabric extending beyond the sections to ¼" seam allowances before joining the sections to make the borders. Add the borders that include the two corners last.

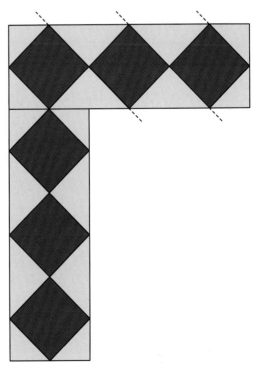

FIGURE 5–22. A TAD PLAID border design (pattern on page 92).

3½"-WIDE BORDER

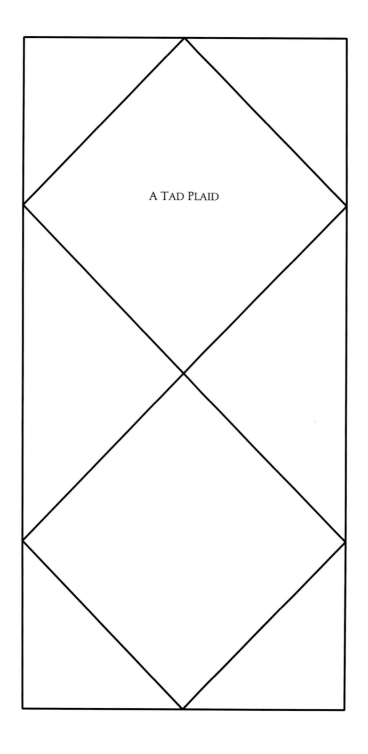

A TAD PLAID

Diamond Border, Sashing, Hot Cotton by Dixie Haywood

Border detail for Hot Cotton, by Dixie Haywood. Full quilt shown on page 74.

DESIGN DETAILS

The 3" sashing and 6" borders are made with the same 3" by 6" unit, pieced in rhomboid-shaped segments. The diamonds are aligned horizontally in the sashing and vertically in the border. The corners are 6" single-fabric squares (Figure 5–23).

To fit the sashing and border to your quilt, enlarge or reduce either the length or the width of the unit. This will change the angle of the diamond.

CONSTRUCTION

1. Prepare border foundations the length of each sashing and border.

2. Cut the fabric with rough-cut templates (page 22). Note that, although the diamonds are identical, the background triangles are oriented differently in the sashing and the border, and they cannot be substituted for each other. The border triangle is half the size of the diamond across the short measurement, and the sashing triangle is half the size of the diamond across the long measurement.

3. Cut the border into piecing segments and sew with under pressed-piecing. It is fast and easy to chain-stitch the segments before cutting, pressing, and adding the next patch.

4. Trim the fabric extending beyond the segments to a ¼" seam allowance before sewing the segments together to make the sashing and the border. Sew the corners to both ends of the last two borders before attaching them to the quilt.

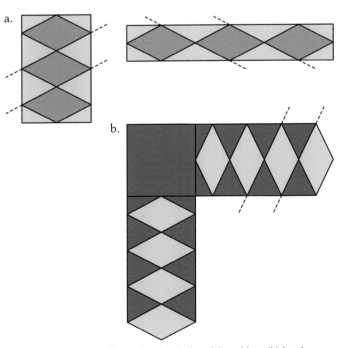

FIGURE 5–23. Hot Cotton border design: (a) sashing, (b) border.

3"-WIDE SASHING
6"-WIDE BORDER

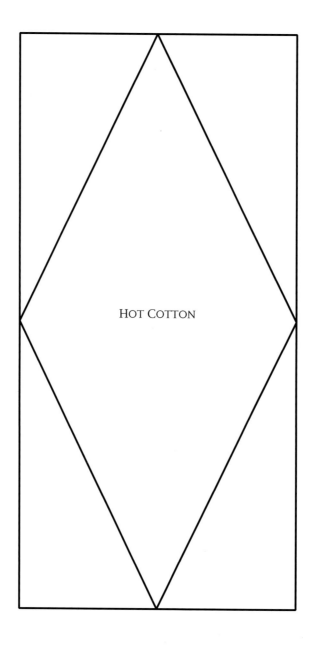

Hot Cotton

CHAPTER 6
Blocks and Built-in Borders

As you can see, it's possible to make a lifetime's worth of quilts with traditional border patterns and innovative variations of them. Borders can be made of shapes from the body of your quilt to reinforce or to provide a contrast with the quilt design, and the use of color can change the graphics of familiar patterns to give them a new look to make your quilt special.

Many other possibilities exist. You needn't look further for a border design than the blocks within your quilt. You may have already done that to repeat shapes in your border, but the exciting potential for bordering a quilt goes beyond the patch shapes to the blocks themselves. The blocks may be changed in size or color from those used in the quilt. They may be halved, quartered, or divided into other segments. It is possible to color a block so that it creates the feel of a border while retaining the patterning of the quilt block. Extending blocks into the border, completing a secondary design where two blocks meet, using a partial block, or recoloring a whole block to frame a quilt are excellent options to consider and explore. We have collected some

examples of quilts in which these concepts have been used successfully, to inspire you to explore new options for your own quilts.

BLOCKS

Eileen Sullivan pieced TRIBUTE TO THE MERCHANTS' MALL from her large selection of blue and brown fabrics, which were bought every time she went near a quilt fabric vendor (Photo 6–1, page 96). She did not have enough of any one fabric for long borders, so she used what she had in limited amounts, breaking into the border with design elements from the quilt top. Extending the diagonal sashing over the multiple strip outer border avoids having the design stop abruptly at the edge of the quilt top. To assess the impact of this simple, eyecatching border, picture the quilt without it.

For another border possibility, use what is usually seen only as a quilt block. Laurie Berdahl's NAUTICAL JOURNEYS AND DOLPHIN DREAMS. was made as a gift for her daughter, who was going into the U.S. Navy (Photo 6–2, page 96). Its nautical theme is composed of sailing ships and leaping

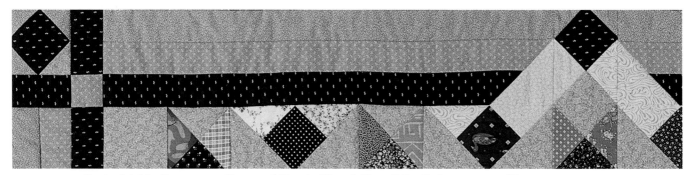

PHOTO 6–1. Border detail for TRIBUTE TO THE MERCHANTS' MALL, by Eileen Sullivan. Full quilt shown on page 97.

PHOTO 6–2. Border detail for NAUTICAL JOURNEYS AND DOLPHIN DREAMS, by Laurie Berdahl. Full quilt top shown on page 9.

PHOTO 6–3a. THE LILY, 5" border squares by Lynn Graves.

PHOTO 6–3b. THE LILY, 5" border squares by Lynn Graves.

porpoises on a blue sea, enhanced by the wave-like curving design of a Snail's Trail border made from fabrics within the quilt. Although the block is used nowhere else in the quilt, it fits with the theme of her quilt perfectly. This block is given as a pattern at the end of the chapter, on page 106.

Lynn Graves, who uses the precise top pressed-piecing technique exclusively, has designed several borders with traditional blocks and shares her Lily border pattern on page 108. Two arrangements of the pattern are shown. One is set straight, creating triangular shapes with radiating points. The other forms a zigzag outline, which could be pointed inward or outward (Photos 6–3a and b).

The promise shown by this block pattern is certainly a reason to look through a quilt block encyclopedia when searching for pieced border ideas. There are many whole or partial patterns, not usually thought of for borders, that could be used in this way. They beg the question of what is a block and what is a border. The answer is they are whatever works best to solve a design challenge.

TRIBUTE TO THE MERCHANTS' MALL, 62" x 98", by Eileen Sullivan.

a.

b.

PHOTO 6–4. Card Trick border, blocks by Dixie Haywood, (a) traditional, (b) variation.

NAUTICAL JOURNEYS AND DOLPHIN DREAMS, by Laurie Berdahl, clipper ships pattern by Stephanie Martin Glennon, corner detail, full quilt shown on page 9.

FIGURE 6–1. Half-blocks set with large plain fabric triangles.

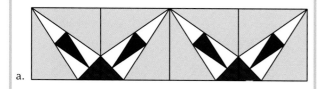

a.

b.

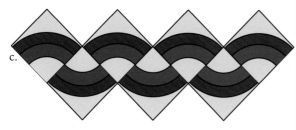

c.

FIGURE 6–2. Blocks with directional patterns: (a) Signal Lights, (b) Palm Leaf, (c) Fan.

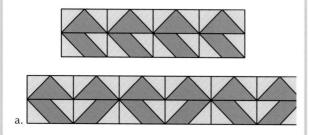

a.

b.

FIGURE 6–3. Potential block-border arrangements: (a) Brown Goose variations, (b) Mrs. Taft's Choice variations.

Card Trick is a whole-block pattern that has potential for an interesting border (Photo 6–4). The shapes within the block are compatible with many quilt designs, and it offers a variety of color and fabric arrangements. Each block is divided into four segments, but with chain piecing, this border can be quickly and easily constructed. A variation of this pattern repeats the interlocking shapes in a continuous design. A full-sized pattern for the block, with diagrams of variations, is given at the end of this chapter on pages 110–111.

Portions of blocks can be positioned at different angles, dovetailing and creating interesting secondary patterns. Blocks that retain their impact when divided diagonally can also be set with alternating plain large triangles (Figure 6–1). Directional patterns used for a border will form zigzag lines around the quilt (Figure 6–2). It may be necessary to drop out or even rearrange some patches to achieve the look you want. Details that are effective in a block may be too cluttered in a border.

Half- and quarter-blocks can be used in different orientations in the same manner as Sawtooth and Flying Geese borders. They can be aligned in the same direction around the quilt or set in pairs along the border, or the direction can be changed in the middle of the border (Figure 6–3).

Patterns consisting of squares can be stretched

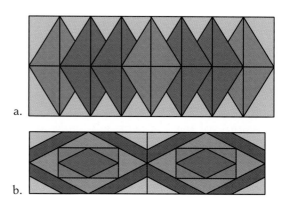

a.

b.

FIGURE 6–4. Stretched blocks: (a) Cascading Diamonds, (b) Depression Block.

PHOTO 6–5. Border detail for BORDEAUX STAR, by Jane Hall. Full quilt shown below.

into rectangles with useful and interesting effects (Figure 6–4). The shapes turn into diamonds, with the angle of the diamond depending on the degree of stretch. One advantage of rectangular blocks is that they make it possible to maintain a unit size while widening the border.

Jane made BORDEAUX STAR by using an off-center, seven-pointed Mariner's Compass design taken from an inlaid floor at La Maison du Vin, in Bordeaux, France (Photo 6–5). She used half-blocks of compasses to surround the center design on three sides, with full blocks at the corners. The bottom border, anchoring the quilt, is a random-pieced string design, made by using dark fabrics from the quilt.

Log Cabin and Pineapple patterns and their infinite variations are natural designs to consider for borders. Their linear composition on several planes makes a strong frame. They can be used classically, in whole or partial blocks. They can also be effectively stretched and re-shaped to conform to the size of border needed.

Claudia Clark Myers gives a contemporary interpretation of the Victorian silk quilts with her flamboyant use of Log Cabin variations (Photo 6–6, page 100). She pieced TWENTIETH CENTURY SILKIE as a center medallion design with four different pieced borders whose shapes shift between circles, triangles, and squares. The center is a traditional Log

Cabin-Pineapple variation, with the light fabrics being repeated in the first border. Subsequent borders of Courthouse Steps, off-center Log Cabins, and triangular Log Cabins are made with the same colors and fabrics used in the dark and light areas to provide continuity in both design and color. Ending with the triangular design creates a radiating-point frame that is very effective. Claudia shares the pattern for her triangle Log Cabin border on pages 114–116.

BORDEAUX STAR, 75" x 46", by Jane Hall.

BUILT-IN BORDERS

When Dixie started making Pineapple quilts, her husband observed that "the pattern never ends." To show him that it could, she started building a border into the blocks at the edge of her quilts. We both often do this by piecing outside portions of the final blocks with a single fabric, creating a solid-appearing border with the texture of the pieced block. Jane did this with NEBULA, so that the pattern was complete and contained with-in the multiple single-fabric borders (see photo on page 37). Dixie floated the stars in both TUITTI-FRUITTI and SPACE LIGHTS the same way (see photos on page 38 and page 43),

There are many variations of this theme. In WEBSITE, Dixie used a spider-web image in the outer blocks and pieced the corners of the block with fabric from the final border (Photo 6–7). This technique maintains the web shape and gives the wide final border a more interesting configuration.

PHOTO 6–6. Border detail for TWENTIETH CENTURY SILKIE, by Claudia Clark Myers. Full quilt shown on page 101.

PHOTO 6–7. Border detail for WEBSITE, by Dixie Haywood. From the collection of Richard and Carla Eaton. Full quilt shown on page 101.

PHOTO 6–8. Border detail for UNTITLED, by Dixie Haywood. Full quilt shown on page 101. PHOTO: MELLISA KARLIN MAHONEY

In UNTITLED, Dixie uses a pieced Pineapple block as a first border with four different traditional Hawaiian appliqué Pineapple blocks (Photo 6–8). The nontraditional color arrangement provides a lot of bang for the buck (Figure 6–5). It expands the background area of the appliqué, provides both a small feathered diamond to repeat the fabric of the appliqué, and makes a transition to the single-fabric border with one of the colors from that fabric. Piecing the fabric of the final border in the corner of the Pineapple block points that border back into the quilt with evenly spaced dog-tooth shapes.

Vicki Doolittle formed her borders entirely with two rows of pieced Pineapple blocks in different values, to create an elaborate frame for her BROMELIAD IN BLOOM (Photo 6–9, page 102). She colored an inner border with two pale fabrics, extending the quilt background into this border. Putting dark turquoise strips on two diagonal planes and in the center of the outer row of blocks made a diagonal design, effectively surrounded by light halos.

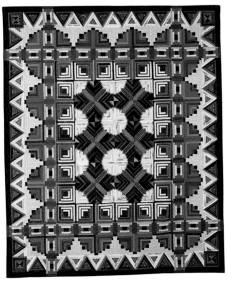

TWENTIETH CENTURY SILKIE, 81" x 101", by Claudia Clark Myers.

WEBSITE, 53" x 53", by Dixie Haywood.
From the collection of Richard and Carla Eaton.

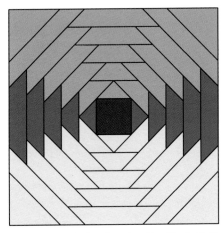

FIGURE 6–5. Pineapple block coloration (See Photo 6–8).

UNTITLED, 62" x 62", by Dixie Haywood. PHOTO: MELLISA KARLIN MAHONEY

Kinko Spencer's SPRING IN THE AIR also has a built-in border made from a partial block (Photo 6–10). Her husband used his computer to help her design and fit the rectangular Pineapple blocks, which were colored to create a strong frame for the pineapple stars in the quilt (Figure 6–6). The corner squares join horizontal and vertical planes of adjacent blocks, making a smooth and easy turning.

Bonnie Rosenbaum, who also designs patterns for precise top piecing, combines four blocks of an off-center Pineapple pattern to create a dramatic star block. It is set in an unusual combination with plain blocks in ANASAZI STAR II (Photo 6–11). For the border, she used rotated pairs of off-center Pineapple blocks, with the same color placement, using the design from the quilt in half- and three-

PHOTO 6–9. Border detail for BROMELIAD IN BLOOM, by Victoria Doolittle. Full quilt shown on page 103.

PHOTO 6–10. Border detail for SPRING IN THE AIR, by Kinko Spencer. Full quilt shown on page 103.

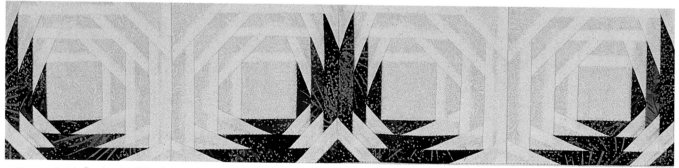

PHOTO 6–11. Border detail for ANASAZI STAR II, by Bonnie Jean Rosenbaum. Full quilt shown on page 103.

quarter images. To separate the border from the quilt and to retain the exact fit, she inserted a single-fabric inner border the size of one block. Bonnie shares her pattern for this block on page 118.

Blocks and designs from within the quilt can be resized, repositioned, or recolored to make a frame that relates to the center design. Creating a border by changing the color of an original quilt block was masterfully done in Rachel Wetzler's A MATTER OF PERSPECTIVE (Photo 6–12, page 104). This dramatic border was created by rearranging the block coloring at the edge of the quilt to repeat colors from the center blocks. She says, "Once the complete quilt design was drawn, I made photocopies and used a soft black pencil to create value drawings. This value play was fascinating because I saw so many possibilities for different quilts or borders – all from the same design – determined strictly by value emphasis." Any additional border on this show-stopper would be superfluous.

CALIFORNIA REEL, made by Allison Lockwood, is a study in how a visual border can be built into a quilt. The border was formed by a change of value or color in the last row of the quilt top (Photo 6–13, page 104). The design gives an entirely new look to the traditional Virginia Reel pattern, also

BROMELIAD IN BLOOM, 48" x 48", by Victoria Doolittle.

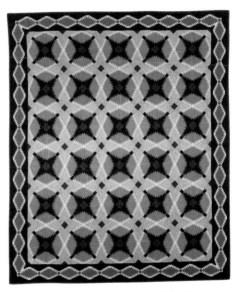

SPRING IN THE AIR, 70" x 72", by Kinko Spencer.

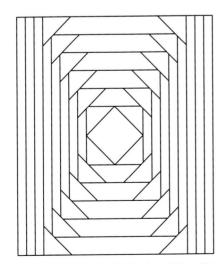

FIGURE 6–6. Rectangular Pineapple block variation. Note added logs on two sides.

ANASAZI STAR II, 54" x 54", by Bonnie Jean Rosenbaum.

known as Snail's Trail. The quilt contains both 4" and 8" blocks set on-point. The strongly colored blocks from the center are mirrored in paler tones at the outside of the quilt. Where they extend to the edge of the quilt, the space between is filled with half-square triangles that create a subtle Dog-tooth as the final edge. Her confidence in letting that light edge finish the quilt is an indication of her sure control of color and design.

Whether using traditional patterns or her own foundation-pieced designs, Eileen Sullivan often merges quilt top and border boundaries by extending blocks into borders. In her artful quilt REMEMBERING MONET, the large flowers and panels of light flow over the inside edge of the dark border at the bottom and left side, while the quilt is contained more rigidly on the right side and at the top (Photo 6–14). The extension of image and color into the

PHOTO 6–12. Border detail for A MATTER OF PERSPECTIVE, by Rachel Wetzler. Full quilt shown on page 105.

PHOTO 6–13. Border detail for CALIFORNIA REEL, by Allison Lockwood. Full quilt shown on page 105.

PHOTO 6–14. Border detail for REMEMBERING MONET, by Eileen Sullivan. Full quilt shown on page 105. PHOTO: MELLISA KARLIN MAHONEY

border area creates a unity to the quilt that a more defined frame would not.

As you design your own quilt, think of the border as part of the whole, and explore the possible choices you can make. Expand beyond the usual single-fabric border and open your mind and eyes to the new horizons a pieced border can offer that will make your quilt noteworthy.

Whether you opt for a simple no-math design, a combination of traditional geometric shapes, or a border suggested by the content of your quilt, the use of foundations will make precise piecing easier. The ability to mark color and piecing order on a foundation will make color and fabric placement goof-proof, and the stability that foundations give will calm any concern about the ultimate fit. Go forth and sew!

A MATTER OF PERSPECTIVE, 46" x 46", by Rachel Wetzler.

CALIFORNIA REEL, 88" x 88", by Allison Lockwood.

REMEMBERING MONET, 58" x 50", by Eileen Sullivan.
PHOTO: MELLISA KARLIN MAHONEY

Snail's Trail from NAUTICAL JOURNEYS AND DOLPHIN DREAMS by Laurie Berdahl

Border detail for NAUTICAL JOURNEYS AND DOLPHIN DREAMS, by Laurie Berdahl. Full quilt shown on page 9.

DESIGN DETAILS

This 5" whole-foundation block forms a border of wave-like images. See also TRAILING THE SNAIL (page 37) and CALIFORNIA REEL (page 105) for variations in block and border designs. To make a continuous-wave design, it is necessary to rotate each block a quarter-turn when joining them (Figure 6–7).

To fit the block to your border, adjust the size of the block.

CONSTRUCTION

1. Prepare block foundations and mark the colors on the foundations to avoid confusion while piecing.

2. Cut fabric for the half-square triangles by using quick-cutting techniques.

3. Use under pressed-piecing to sew all the triangles to the foundation.

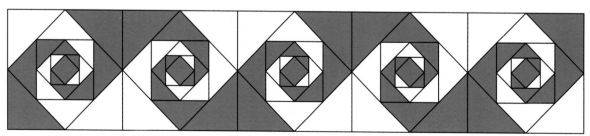

FIGURE 6–7. SNAIL'S TRAIL border variation (pattern on page 107).

5" BLOCK

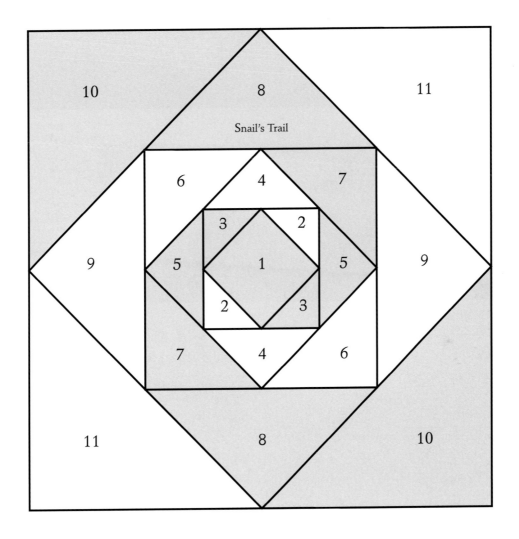

The Lily, by Lynn Graves

The Lily, version 1, 5" border squares by Lynn Graves.

The Lily, version 2, 5" border squares by Lynn Graves.

DESIGN DETAILS

These borders are made by using a 5" finished-sized square with one flower section from the traditional North Carolina Lily block (Figure 6–8). Version 1 has two matched pairs of flower sections separated by a spacer strip, with an optional second row of large triangles containing the lily design.

Version 2 has rotated pairs of squares, sewn to each other without spacers. To fit Border 1 to your quilt, adjust the width of the spacers, which will determine the size of the large quarter-square triangles on either side of the block in the second row. To fit Border 2 to your quilt, adjust the size of the block to the unit needed.

a.

spacer

b.

FIGURE 6–8. The Lily border design by Lynn Graves: (a) version 1, (b) version 2.

The Lily

CONSTRUCTION

(Precise top pressed-piecing, page 19)

1. Prepare the needed number of foundations.

2. Cut the fabric pieces for the block.

3. Cut spacers and quarter-square triangles as needed to fit your quilt.

4. Piece blocks by using precise top pressed-piecing. Remember, the lines are fabric placement lines and trimming lines, not sewing lines. You will be stitching ¼" to the left of each line. The foundation includes the ¼" seam allowance. Trim excess fabric on the outer edge of the foundation.

First row

Piece 1, cut a scant 3" square.

Pieces 2, 3, 4 and 5, cut 2¾" squares once diagonally.

Piece 6, cut a strip 2¼" wide.

Piece 7, cut a 3½" square once diagonally.

Second row

Cut quarter-square triangles as needed to fit your quilt.

5" BLOCK

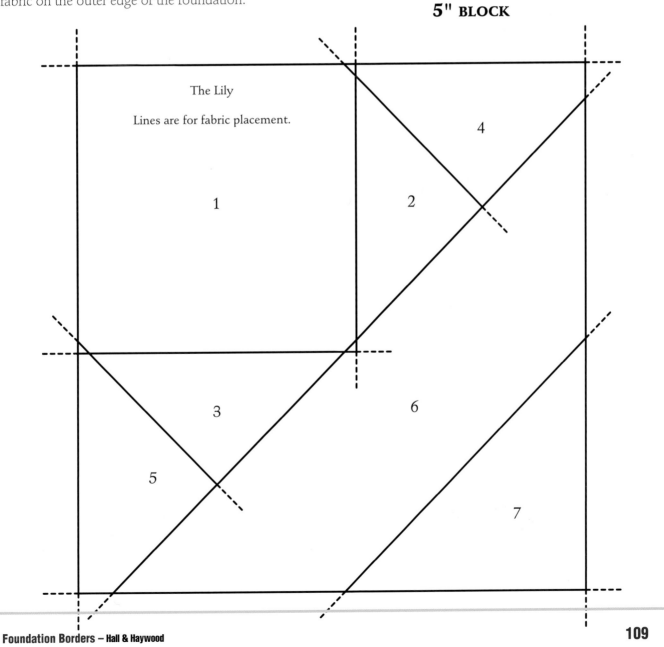

The Lily

Lines are for fabric placement.

Card Trick, Card Trick blocks by Dixie Haywood

a.

b.

Card Trick border, blocks by Dixie Haywood, (a) traditional, (b) variation.

DESIGN DETAILS

This 6" segmented block can be combined to form a border of double-interlocked shapes, with many design and color options (Figure 6–9).

To fit this border to your quilt, adjust the size of the block, or stretch it into a rectangle. Depending on how the rectangle is pieced in the border, it can widen the border or lengthen the units.

CONSTRUCTION

1. To make the traditional design, prepare the number of block foundations needed for the quilt. Cut them in segments. This block requires two different foundation segments, each repeated twice. To avoid confusion, it is essential to write color choices on the foundations and to lay out the fabric patches as they will be pieced. If a color progression extends into the border from the quilt body, piece the blocks one at a time.

2. Cut the fabric for the triangles by using quick-cutting techniques. The large triangles are half-square triangles. The small ones are quarter-square triangles.

3. Use under pressed-piecing to sew the fabric pieces to the foundations.

4. To make the variation, follow the same steps but note that some lines have been dropped out. The segments and piecing order are different.

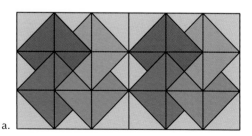

a.

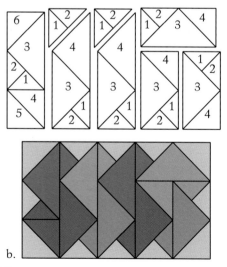

b.

FIGURE 6–9. Card Trick border design (pattern on page 111), (a) traditional, (b) variation.

6" BLOCK

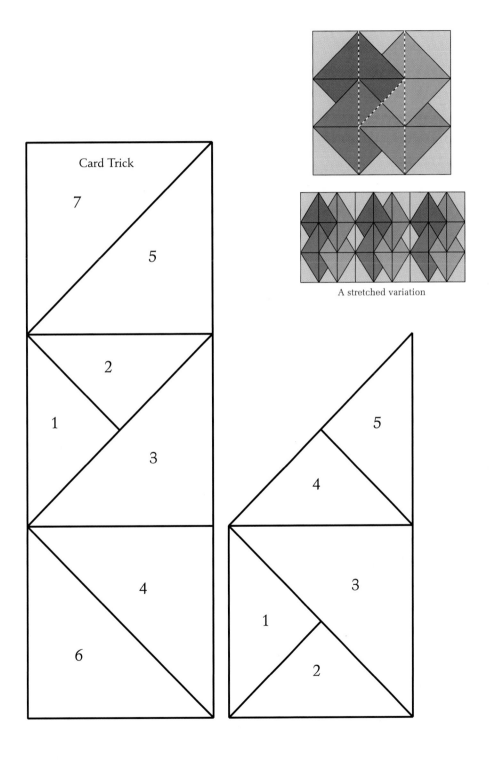

A stretched variation

Card Trick

Half Mariner's Compass

Border detail for BORDEAUX STAR, by Jane Hall. Full quilt shown on page 99.

DESIGN DETAILS

The border of Bordeaux Star contains half-blocks of the seven-pointed Mariner's Compass design in the quilt, with whole blocks at the corners (Figure 6–10). The pieced blocks were appliquéd onto plain fabric borders. The background fabric was then cut from behind the appliqués, and the foundations were removed.

To fit this border to your quilt, adjust the size of the block or add spacer strips around the edge of the quilt.

CONSTRUCTION

1. Prepare the number of block foundations needed for the border by tracing the whole pattern. Add the letter labels to the pieces.

2. Cut the foundation into segments. For each half-block, you will need four As, two half-Cs, and three C-B-C wedge segments.

3. Cut fabric for the B and C points with rough-cut templates. (Use a standard ¼" seam allowance for B and ⅜" seam allowances for the C wedges.)

4. Piece using single foundation piecing for the A and half-C segments and under pressed-piecing

for the C-B-C wedges. Assemble the points with the wedges, matching the cut-edges of the freezer-paper foundations, to form the blocks. Some seams will be set-in.

FIGURE 6–10. Half Mariner's Compass border design (pattern on page 113).

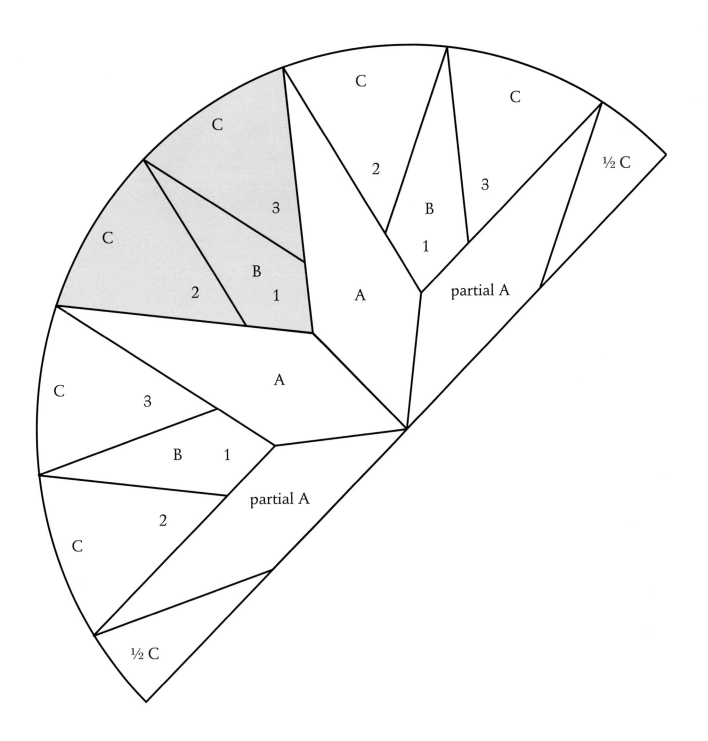

Triangular Log Cabin, from TWENTIETH CENTURY SILKIE by Claudia Clark Myers

Border detail for TWENTIETH CENTURY SILKIE, by Claudia Clark Myers. Full quilt shown on page 101.

DESIGN DETAILS

This 6" triangular border block in TWENTIETH CENTURY SILKIE is made from two sizes of strips (Figure 6–11). The same center fabric is used in the blocks, which are alternately light and dark along the border with a half block at each end. A Log Cabin block or a single-fabric square the color of the block centers makes an appropriate corner for this border. Notice that, in Claudia's quilt, an inner Courthouse Steps border frames the quilt in a lattice design, which crosses over into the final two borders.

To fit the border to your quilt, enlarge or reduce the block or add strips to it.

CONSTRUCTION

1. Prepare foundations for the blocks, half blocks, and corners. The half-blocks at the ends of each border are mirror images, so half of those foundations must be reversed. Mark the color placement on the foundations.

2. Cut a center triangle, adding ¼" seam allowance on all sides, and cut narrow strips ½" and wide strips 1".

3. Using under pressed-piecing, sew the blocks and join them into border lengths. The foundations include ¼" seam allowances, so trim the fabric to the line after the blocks have been sewn.

FIGURE 6–11. Adaptation of Triangular Log Cabin border design by Claudia Clark Myers (patterns on pages 115 and 116).

6" TRIANGLE

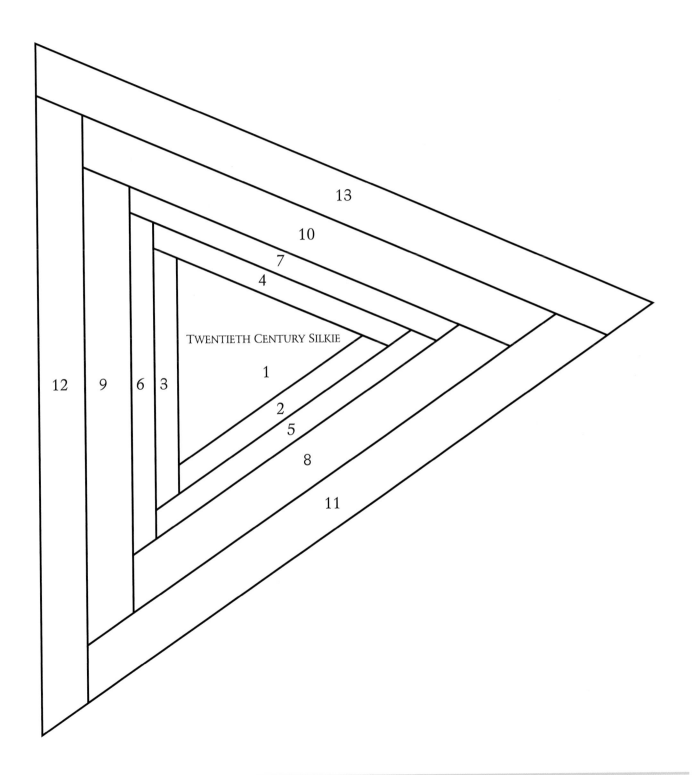

TWENTIETH CENTURY SILKIE

Triangular Log Cabin, from Twentieth Century Silkie by Claudia Clark Myers

6" HALF-TRIANGLE

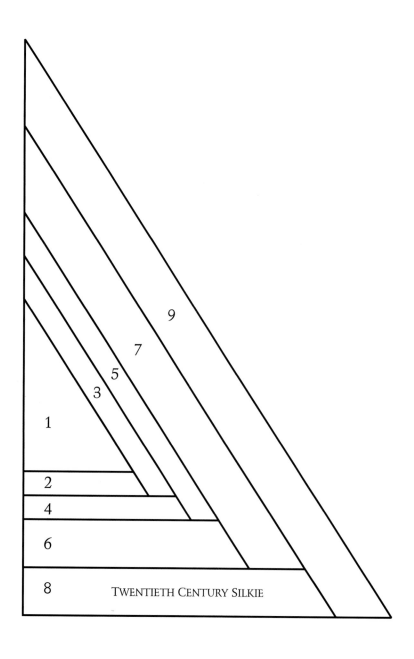

9
7
5
3
1
2
4
6
8

TWENTIETH CENTURY SILKIE

Off-Center Pineapple, ANASAZI STAR II by Bonnie Jean Rosenbaum

Border detail for ANASAZI STAR II, by Bonnie Jean Rosenbaum. Full quilt shown on page 103.

DESIGN DETAILS

This 4½" off-center Pineapple block forms a star when four blocks are combined (see ANASAZI STAR II on page 103). Two blocks rotated and joined make a half-star for the border, which complements the quilt design and turns the corner smoothly. The block contains two sizes of strips. The narrow ones in the horizontal and vertical planes are cut from dark fabrics, and all other strips, both wide and narrow, are cut from the background fabric (Figure 6–12).

To fit the border to your quilt, enlarge or reduce the size of the block, or add another row of strips to the block. The pattern as given includes a ¼" seam allowance on all sides, which must be taken into account if you alter the dimensions.

CONSTRUCTION

(Precise top pressed-piecing, page 19)

1. Prepare foundations for the blocks and mark the color notations on the foundations.

2. Cut the fabric pieces for the blocks. Cut center squares a scant 2" and strips 1" and 1¼". Cut triangle #25 from a 2" square cut in half diago-nally. Cut triangle #26 from a 1¾" square cut in half diagonally.

3. Stitch the foundations by using precise top pressed-piecing. Remember that the pattern lines are for fabric placement, not stitching. You will always be stitching ¼" to the left of the line. Trim any excess fabric after each seam so the fabric placement line is visible before positioning the next piece.

FIGURE 6–12. Off-center Pineapple design by Bonnie Jean Rosenbaum (pattern on page 118).

4½" BLOCK

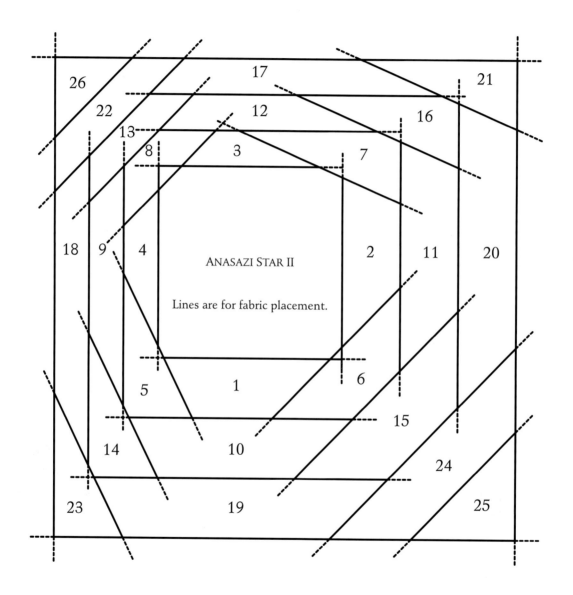

ANASAZI STAR II

Lines are for fabric placement.

Contributing Artists

TOUCAN TANGO, shown on page 70.

Jennifer Amor, Columbia, South Carolina, is a nationally known teacher, designer, and author who specializes in wearable art, non-traditional techniques, machine cutwork, and bargello. She has introduced thousands of children to quilting through her artist-in-education residencies and her book *Flavor Quilts for Kids to Make* (American Quilter's Society, 1991). She firmly believes that quilting should be fun for adults and children alike.

JOHN'S MICHIGAN MEMORIES, shown on pages 14, 66, and 67.

Debra Ballard, Midland, Michigan, cannot remember a time when quilts were not part of her life. Her grandmother and great-grandmother were quilters, and she herself has been quilting ever since she took a quilting class in 1984. Her award-winning quilts have been exhibited in quilt shows and many publications. She teaches and lectures for guilds and shops and focuses primarily on appliqué for both beginners and the more advanced. She believes it is important to learn different methods because "all techniques are tools in our sewing baskets."

NAUTICAL JOURNEYS AND DOLPHIN DREAMS, shown on pages 8, 9, 96, 97, and 106.

Laurie Berdahl, Pensacola, Florida, began quilting eight years ago, having retired from the U.S. Navy. She was stationed in Okinawa with time on her hands, and with 20 plus years of sewing experience, she immediately and easily took to quiltmaking basics. She gravitated toward miniature quilts because of her "guilt at wasting scraps" and her desire to see just how small she could go with a block. Laurie says, "I love the classic patterns but am always looking to add a new twist on them to give a quilt some punch."

KATHERINE CONNOR'S WHEELS, shown on pages 64 and 65.

Kathy Butts, Merlin, Oregon, had quilts from her family but had never made one until 1988 when she and her mother made a Log Cabin entirely by hand. Then she saw a quilting program on TV, demonstrating rotary cutting, and, as she says, "The rest is history." She has worked in stained glass, which her quilts sometimes reflect. For the past few years, she has designed her own versions of traditional quilts, and all her free time now revolves around quiltmaking. She and her husband owned a woodworking shop and sold wooden novelties and music boxes nationwide until they retired.

FOOD QUILT: IN MY GRANDMOTHER'S KITCHEN, shown on page 63.

Susan Dague, Piedmont, California, learned to quilt from a housemate in Atlanta, Georgia, in the early 1970s. She moved to California where she worked at a local fabric store, took quilting classes, and began to create quilts…more than 50 so far. She took a foundation piecing class from Dixie and Jane in 1994 and has used foundation piecing extensively since then. Her work features traditional patterns made from both vintage and modern fabrics.

CALYPSO, shown on pages 66 and 67.

Susan Derkacz, New Braunfels, Texas, has been quilting for 25 years. She enjoys making quilts as bed covers as well as art forms and has won many awards for her designs. She loves hand appliqué compositions. Susan's current interest is making contemporary quilts based on traditional designs.

BROMELAID IN BLOOM, shown on pages 102 and 103.

Victoria Doolittle, Third Lake, Illinois, has been quilting for 26 years and is self-taught. Her specialties are English paper piecing, Pineapple designs, and crazy quilting. She also collects pre 1950s sewing machines, mostly Singers, and has around 55 or so. She teaches and lectures and will start lecturing about the machines soon. She says, "I think the machines are more my passion than quilting."

TRAILING THE SNAIL, shown on pages 36, 37, and 51.

Linda Erickson, Albuquerque, New Mexico, has been involved in sewing and crafts since high school and taught herself to quilt about 12 years ago. She enjoys taking workshops with visiting quilt instructors and is still exploring different styles of quiltmaking and quilt design. Linda makes many quilts for the New Mexico Quilters' Association's Sweet Charity group and has won awards in statewide shows.

WANDERING FANS, shown on page 41.

Brooke Flynn, Billings, Montana, learned to quilt at the YWCA in Billings in the mid 1970s. She used polyester fabric, templates made from cereal boxes, and patterns run on a mimeograph machine. Even then, the process was fascinating and satisfying. She and her family now operate the Flynn Quilt Frame Company and teach and lecture at quilt conferences.

THE LILY, shown on pages 96 and 108.

Lynn Graves, Chama, New Mexico, known as "the Little Foot lady," says that "quilting found me in January 1985. It quickly became my passion and magnificent obsession." This obsession led Lynn to design tools and foundations to help with her own quilting skills, which has become a business that has acquired a world-wide following. In November 1999, the family and business moved to Chama where they also host quilt retreats.

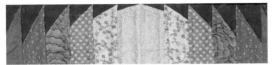
SAGAN'S SUNRISE, shown on pages 66 and 68.

Bette Haddon, DeFuniak Springs, Florida, has reinvented her quilt persona from a "purist" traditional quilter, working by hand, to an art quilter, focusing on art quilts with "energy, color gradation, and dimension" and outstanding machine quilting. Her new direction has been recognized with many awards. Bette's experience includes owning a quilt shop in Ft. Wayne, Indiana, in the 1980s, and teaching arts and crafts aboard a cruise line in the 1990s, which opened the world to her.

CRAZY QUILT FOR A CRAZY KID, shown on page 30.

Delores Hamilton, Cary, North Carolina, has two adult children and adores two Siamese cats. She became a full-time quilter in 2001 after an early retirement. Her love affair with color began in the fifth grade when she chose fuchsia and lime angora sweaters and socks. Her grandmother started her on needle arts when she was four, but she set aside all of those when she discovered quilting in 1988. Now, with gusto, she throws fuchsia and lime, and every other color, into her quilts. Fortunately, those genes passed down to her son, who requested "a mass of colors" for his quilt.

RED FEATHERS, shown on pages 66 and 67.

Lynne G. Harrill, Jesup, Georgia, has been making quilts since the late 1970s. Her sewing experience began in childhood, and by high school, she was sewing clothes professionally. Before becoming a full-time studio fiber artist, she was a public school teacher. Lynne is a juried member of the Southern Highland Craft Guild and a professional member of Studio Art Quilt Associates.

CALIFORNIA REEL, shown on pages 11, 13, 104, and 105.

Allison Lockwood, Shell Beach, California, has a degree in psychology from the University of California, San Diego. Her quilting journey began with baby quilts, prior to the arrival of her second daughter in 1986. Allison's works are primarily bold interpretations of traditional blocks that are foundation pieced and hand quilted. Her quilts have been published in magazines, books, and calendars, and they have been exhibited across the United States, Japan, and Europe.

TWENTIETH CENTURY SILKIE, shown on pages 12, 13, 100, 101, and 114.

Claudia Clark Myers, Duluth, Minnesota, comes to the quilt world with 25 years experience as a costume designer for the Baltimore Opera Company; Minnesota Ballet; A. T. Jones Costumers in

Baltimore, Maryland; and Malabar Costume House in Toronto, Canada. She taught costume design and construction in the theater department at the College of St. Scholastica. She has had numerous quilts juried into national shows and has won awards at many of them. Claudia and her business partner, Barb Engelking, have started a quilt pattern business called 2 Much Fun.

AUTUMN GARDEN GLORY, shown on pages 24 and 25.

Marge Nickels, Germantown, Tennessee, has a background in dressmaking and tailoring, and she has been sewing clothes for herself since age 11. Her quiltmaking adventure started in 1987 with some basic quilting classes. Her emphasis is on using traditional patterns in contemporary colors and contrasts to create surprises in the piece. Her day job as an accountant provides the means to support her quilting habit, while the quilting provides welcome relief from numbers. Marge loves to quilt, garden, cook, golf, and spend time at home with her husband and two cats.

RAINBOWS IN THE SNOW, shown on page 35.
ANASAZI STAR II, shown on pages 102, 103, and 117.

Bonnie Jean Rosenbaum, Albuquerque, New Mexico, a quilter since 1978, started doing quilting demonstrations at the state fair that year, and soon after, began teaching machine piecing at local quilt shops. She specializes in miniature quilts, and her framed miniatures have been entered into several juried shows and have won many awards. Bonnie's quilts and patterns can often be seen in miniature-quilt magazines, and she has won ribbons each year in Chitra's Miniatures from the Heart Contest. She began to produce her own line of miniature paper-foundation sheet patterns in 1990.

GOLDEN TWILIGHT, shown on page 71.

Marlene Royse, Raleigh, North Carolina, began sewing before the age of six and soon received her first sewing machine, a Singer Sew-Handy hand-crank, chain-stitch machine, which she used to make doll clothes. She has been sewing ever since. She began quilting in the early 1970s and enjoys taking classes from many teachers, gleaning techniques and ideas to facilitate construction of her designs. She loves antique quilts and, because of fabric and block selection, most of her quilts look as if they might have been made many years ago.

SAMARKAND, shown on page 63.

Virginia Siciliano, Centereach, New York, has been quilting for more than 20 years. She enjoys using traditional patterns in unique ways. This award-winning quilter finds that color selection and placement, fabric choice, and hand quilting are the most exciting aspects of the quilting process. Virginia shares her quilt studio with her husband, George, who is a quilt artist specializing in miniatures.

SPRING IN THE AIR, shown on pages 102 and 103.

JEWETT, NATURE AT ITS BEST, shown on pages 30 and 31.

Kinko Spencer, Raleigh, North Carolina, has been sewing since childhood. After her last child left home, she began looking for a new hobby and began quilting in 1987. She is self-taught. Most of her quilts are traditionally based, but several of her wallhangings are her own design. She especially likes to design borders. Her husband has helped her tremendously by drafting them on his computer. Her color choices are influenced by her native country, Japan.

Betty Verhoeven, East Jewett, New York, was born and raised in the Netherlands. She never saw a quilt until she moved with her husband to a farm in the Catskill Mountains. Inspired by a neighbor who was making a Cathedral patch quilt, Betty began quilting. Largely self-taught, she started with traditional patterns but was soon designing her own. When the town of Jewett asked her to make a quilt for their sesquicentennial celebration, she collected old photographs from the townspeople, copied them on rose satin fabric, and framed them with foundation-made crazy patch work.

TRIBUTE TO THE MERCHANTS' MALL, shown on pages 10, 11, 96, and 97. REMEMBERING MONET, shown on pages 104 and 105.

Eileen Sullivan, Alpharetta, Georgia, has a degree in art education and has taught art in public schools for eight years. She has been quilting for more than 20 years and has been designing quilts that are foundation pieced on freezer paper since 1988. She is primarily interested in innovative design and exploration of techniques. Her quilts have been exhibited throughout the United States and abroad, and they have been awarded honors in most major competitions. She teaches and lectures nationally in addition to managing her business, The Designer's Workshop.

A MATTER OF PERSPECTIVE, shown on pages 104 and 105.

Rachel Wetzler, St. Charles, Illinois, has sewn and done hand work since childhood, but when she made her first quilt from a stitchery magazine pattern in 1989, she knew at once that quilting was her "thing." After making several quilts from commercial patterns, she ventured into designing her own quilts, which were entered into competition. The meaning and symbolism in the quilts are as important as the design. Each quilt conveys her hope in God and her desire that the viewer be touched by that hope.

Resources

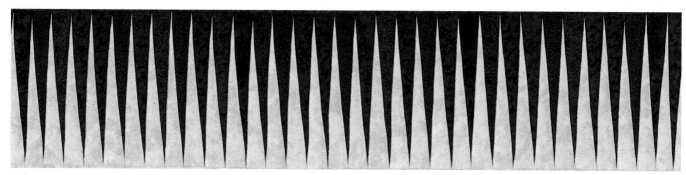

Border detail for INDIGO, 72" x 90", by Jane Hall. Full quilt shown page 61.

Bonnie Jean Rosenbaum
3513 Smith SE
Albuquerque, NM 87106
505-265-5223
bonnierosenbaum@prodigy.net

Miniature paper foundation pieced patterns.

Flynn Quilt Frame Company
1000 Shiloh Overpass Rd.
Billings, MT 59106
800-745-3596
www. flynnquilt.com

No-baste Flynn Multi-Frame quilting system and fine quilting templates, products, and books.

Graphic Impressions
1090 Highpoint Dr.
Nicholasville, KY 40356
859-881-0377

Easy-Tear™, lightweight removable interfacing for foundations; pattern stencils.

Graywood Designs
PO Box 531
Pigeon, MI 48755

Patterns by Debra Ballard.

Hall & Haywood
200 Transylvania Ave.,
Raleigh, NC 27609-6318
jqhall@earthlink.net

Perfect Pineapples book (out of print but available); foundation piecing papers for traditional and off-center pineapple designs.

HQS, Inc.
PO Box 94237
Phoenix, AZ 85070-4237
480-460-3697
www.trianglesonaroll.com

Triangles on a Roll, continuous grids on rolls for constructing half- and quarter-square triangles.

Jennifer Amor Designs
3702 Blossom St.
Columbia, SC 29205
803-256-0146

Flavor Quilts for Kids to Make book, workshops, and the pattern for Toucan Tango (page 70), the first in a series of Happy Quilts.

Karen K. Stone
5418 McCommas Blvd.
Dallas, TX 75206
www.KarenKStone.com

Pine Burr, New York Beauty, and other patterns.

Little Foot LTD
Lynn Graves
PO Box 1027
Chama, NM 87520
www.Littlefoot.net

Paper foundations for precise top pressed-piecing plus tools, including Little Foot.®

Material Possessions Quilt Shop
22600-C Lambert St., Suite 905
Lake Forest, CA 92630
949-586-3418
www.quilt@quiltessentials.com (web site)

Templates and pattern for Wheels of Whimsey (used in KATHERINE CONNOR'S WHEELS), designed by Wendy Hager.

Starry Night Designs
PO Box 1461
Portsmouth, NH 03802

Clipper Ships pattern, designed by Stephanie Martin Glennon.

The Designers Workshop
Eileen Sullivan
PO Box 1026
Duluth, GA 30096
www.Thedesignersworkshop.com

Foundation-pieced patterns for original designs on freezer paper.

2 Much Fun
5715 Jean Duluth Rd.
Duluth, MN 55803
218-525-7764

Paper-pieced patterns, pattern brochure for Claudia Clark Myers designs ($1.00).

Thangles
PO Box 2266
Fond du Lac, WI 54936

Foundations to make half-square triangles from strips.

Vintage Collections
PO Box 171
Sorrento, FL 32776
352-735-4986
www.cindyblackberg.com

Patterns for pieced designs by Cindy Blackberg.

Bibliography

Beyer, Jinny. *The Quilter's Album of Blocks and Borders.* McLean, VA: EPM Publications, 1980.

Brackman, Barbara. *Encyclopedia of Pieced Quilt Patterns.* Paducah, KY: American Quilter's Society, 1993.

Hall, Jane, and Dixie Haywood. *Perfect Pineapples.* Martinez, CA: C&T Publishing, 1989.

——. *Precision Pieced Quilts Using the Foundation Method.* Radnor, PA: Chilton Book Co., 1992.

——. *Firm Foundations.* Paducah, KY: American Quilter's Society, 1996.

——. *Hall & Haywood's Foundation Quilts: Building on the Past.* Paducah, KY; American Quilter's Society, 2000.

Haywood, Dixie. *Crazy Quilting Patchwork.* New York: Dover Publications, 1986.

——. *Quick and Easy Crazy Patchwork.* New York: Dover Publications, 1992.

Johannah, Barbara. *Barbara Johannah's Crystal Piecing.* Radnor, PA: Chilton Book Co., 1993.

Martin, Judy, and Marsha McCloskey. *Pieced Borders.* Grinnell, IA: Crosley-Griffith Publishing Company, Inc., 1994.

Jane Hall and Dixie Haywood

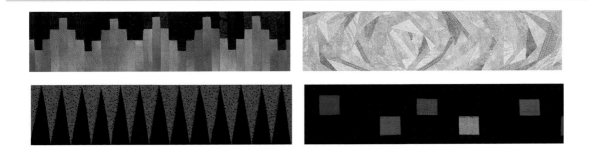

Award-winning quiltmakers and long-time friends Jane Hall and Dixie Haywood began collaborating in 1989. This is their fifth book exploring contemporary applications for the old-made-new technique of foundation piecing. Their goal, both as teachers and authors, is to empower quilters to expand their quilting repertoires with techniques that make their creative efforts trouble-free and precise.

Both Jane and Dixie enjoy working with innovative approaches to traditional designs by using color as a tool to create a new, fresh look. They each work independently on quilts with various designs, most of which are made by foundation piecing.

Jane learned to quilt in Hawaii in the early 1970s and never looked back. She teaches, lectures, judges, and does appraisals for old and new quilts. She lives in Raleigh, North Carolina, with her husband, Bob, and Tilly the cat. They have six children and 10 grandchildren, a few of whom live nearby. They enjoy travel, whether quilt-related or not, especially to France and United Kingdom.

Dixie has been quilting since the late 1960s and has been a teacher, lecturer, designer, and judge on the national scene since the publication of her first book in 1977. She recently retired from teaching but still finds the days are not long enough for all the quilting she wants to do. Dixie lives in Pensacola, Florida, with her husband, Bob. They have two sons, a daughter, three grandsons, and a great-granddaughter. When not quilting, Dixie enjoys yoga and cooking, along with searching for a low-maintenance garden.

Other AQS Books

This is only a small selection of the books available from the American Quilter's Society. AQS books are known worldwide for timely topics, clear writing, beautiful color photos, and accurate illustrations and patterns. The following books are available from your local bookseller, quilt shop, or public library.

#6204   us$19.95

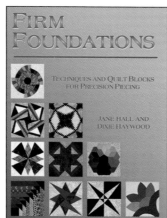

#4594   us$18.95

#6213   us$24.95

#5852   us$19.95

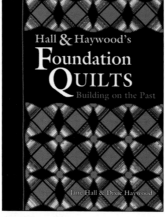

#5707   us$26.95

#5176   us$24.95

#5761   us$22.95

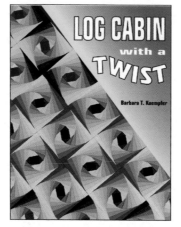

#4545   us$18.95

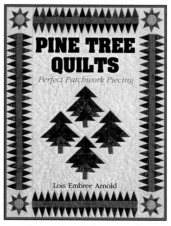

#5708   us$22.95